The Tunesmith & The Lyricist

Vernon Duke, Ira Gershwin and the Making of a Standard

George Harwood Phillips

Coyote Hill Press

Published by Coyote Hill Press, Camano Island, Washington

Layout & Design by Robin S. Hanks

First Edition, 2016

Printed in the United States

ISBN: 978-0-9912641-5-5 All rights reserved.

In memory of
Ira Gershwin and Vernon Duke

Contents

Acknowledgements

I am indebted to several people for reading the manuscript and offering suggestions for its improvement. They include Shelly Guralnick, Natalie Kuhlman, Barry Anderson, Marline Zeiger, and Jack Johnson, who also was instrumental in locating many of the recordings mentioned in the text. Special thanks go to Ira Gershwin biographer Philip Furia and to Michael Owen of the Ira and Leonore S. Gershwin Trusts. They graciously read the manuscript, submitted by me, a stranger, identified errors, and pointed me in new directions. The Trusts also provided photographs that were incorporated as illustrations. Musicians Scott Holden and Aaron Ziegel provided me with articles they had written on Vernon Duke, and the staff of the Music Division of the Library of Congress reproduced for me photographs and the letters of Ira Gershwin to Vernon Duke and those of Duke to Ira and George Gershwin. Your assistance was invaluable.

Finally, thanks to editors Robin and Richard Hanks for whipping the manuscript into fine shape. It was a pleasure working with you.

Preface

This book applies the specific to explain the general. It takes one song, written in the mid 1930s, and uses it to address larger issues regarding popular music in the twentieth century. The song—"I Can't Get Started With You"—is discussed in considerable detail, but so is jazz and its connection with the musical theater, the early lives and collaborations of the song's creators, the nature of lyric writing, the structure of the popular song, the legacy of George Gershwin, the musicians who performed and recorded "I Can't Get Started" (its common title), and the later lives, independent musical contributions, and legacies of Vernon Duke and Ira Gershwin.

This song was chosen because of the many varied and dynamic renditions that it has received from vocalists and instrumentalists during the first decade of its existence. Discussed and analyzed, however, are only those renditions that form distinct chapters in the biography of the song, that serve as benchmarks in the history of jazz, and that demonstrate how vocalists interpreted and changed the lyric—a development that occurred more frequently than with any other song of the period. Because most of the renditions noted in the text are available on 78 rpm records, LPs, and CDs and can be heard on various internet outlets, it is highly recommended that they be listened to as soon as mentioned. Also available on the internet are renditions of many of the other songs identified, as well as scenes from various movies discussed.

Chapter One
Black Music, White Musicals: Intersecting Histories

By about 1900 two distinctly American art forms had developed in the United States—jazz and the musical comedy. Both of them have long and radically different histories that began when Europeans and Africans first arrived in different areas of North America. But in time these two art forms would intersect and influence one another. The composers of musicals would give jazz new songs with which to experiment. The creators of jazz would provide musicals with new harmonies, differentiated melodic lines, and syncopated rhythms. On occasion, jazz musicians provided the music to Broadway shows.

Prior to this intersection, several different kinds of American musical entertainments had spread over much of the East and South during the nineteenth century. With no recognizable European antecedents, minstrelsy was a uniquely American entertainment that emerged in the 1820s. White performers darkened their skins with burnt cork to supposedly look like plantation Blacks and spoke, sang, and danced like black people were supposed to speak, sing, and dance. Minstrelsy, while obviously racist from today's perspective, was thought by most whites and many blacks as well to be innocent entertainment. There were, however, positive aspects of minstrelsy. As troupes toured across the United States, they introduced new songs, some of them becoming what we would today call hits, such as Stephen Foster's "Oh! Susannah," "Camptown Races," "Old Black Joe," "Beautiful Dreamer," and "Old Folks at Home." Another legacy of minstrelsy was its flexible format which allowed for sketches, songs, and dances to be continually updated to fit the tastes of different audiences.[1]

That American vaudeville was influenced by minstrelsy is evident in its flexible format. But it exhibited much more variety in its acts that included acrobats, animal trainers, singers, and dancers. A novelty act such as a sword swallower might be followed by a one-act play sometimes with a famous actor in the lead; it would be followed by headliner who was usually a singer or comedian. As historian John Kendrick has explained, Vaudeville also

> provided a template for the Broadway revues of the early twentieth century. More importantly, vaudeville's comedians, dancers, and singers would play a direct role in reshaping the musical theatre. . . . Two or more shows a day taught performers how to evoke anything from laughter to tears, and competition forced them to grab an audience's attention quickly and hold it as long as possible. Vaudeville's performers and writers had to contend with a nationwide audience, one that stretched far beyond New York's City limits. That is why variety and vaudeville veterans shaped Broadway's earliest musical comedies as populist entertainment aimed at the common man and woman, giving the new, vast working class a cultural voice.[2]

Before that occurred, the Broadway musical went through an important stage. Once the comic operas of Gilbert and Sullivan were performed in New York in the late 1870s and early 1880s, especially *H.M.S. Pinafore, The Pirates of Penzance, Patience,* and *The Mikado,* they became the model for the American musical theater. These and other productions stimulated American composers and lyricists to provide their audiences with more melodic creativity and wit than had previously been the case.[3] But as American writers and producers introduced loose plots and ordinary instead of aristocratic characters into their shows, the need for American-sounding songs increased. Satisfying that need were increasing numbers of songwriters associated with New York publishing firms. Beginning about 1885, many established their businesses on West 28th Street, a section of which became known as Tin Pan

Alley—the clatter of pianos resembling housewives pounding on tin pans. The rationale of Tin Pan Alley was to create popular, often cliche-ridden songs and market them in sheet music to the masses. But some composers who wrote for Tin Pan Alley also wrote for the theater, and publishers often published both popular and theater songs. Thus, the musical theatre and the musical publishing industry became intimately linked. If a song in a show became a hit, it contributed to the selling of the sheet music. And by printing and thereby publicizing the song, the industry enhanced the selling of tickets.[4]

Although the intersection of art and business mainly benefitted the white musical, a few black musicals were staged during the 1890s and early 1900s. *The Creole Show* was performed in New York in 1890 and featured several women in what usually was an all-male cast. It was followed by *A Trip to Coontown* in 1898, the first full-length New York musical comedy created and performed by African Americans. The show was replete with minstrel stereotypes, as was *In Dahomey* produced in 1903. The runs of these shows were short, and the black musical went into hiatus for a decade, only to reemerge with the rise in the popularity of jazz.[5]

As analyzed by Charles Hamm, the musical theater, as it existed at the beginning of the twentieth century, can be placed in a continuum, with opera at one end and vaudeville at the other. In between was a mixed field consisting of operettas and stage productions called musical comedies, musical plays, or plays with music. They consisted of comic characters, dancing, songs, choruses, and ensemble numbers. Continuity of character and plot was generally lacking or given only minimal emphasis. Shows consisting of several different sections or acts became known as follies or revues. "It was here," wrote Hamm, "that the most successful and uniquely American forms of twentieth-century musical theater emerged."[6]

Writing music for a musical comedy or revue was different from writing for vaudeville. An overture was needed, as were songs for the dance sequences, for the chorus, and for individual performers. The style of the song, moreover, changed. In vaudeville, the song was designed for the performer in a sketch in which dialect was often used. The melody was subordinate to the lyric. In a revue, however, the song was designed to showcase a singer's voice.[7] Earlier songs usually dealt with rural life, but in the hands of immigrants and first generation Irish, Italian, and especially Jewish composers the songs spoke of city dwellers, in particular those living in New York.[8] As explained by Deena Rosenberg, the contrasts between "their parents insular past and their own wide-open present" led second generation Jewish light verse poets, humorists, and lyricists to become "acute social observers."[9]

Irving Berlin was one of those observers, and he wrote one of the most influential of the new songs—"Alexander's Ragtime Band." By the end of 1912, two million copies of the sheet music had been sold, its unique structure having much to do with its success. Most but not all popular songs of the nineteenth century emphasized the verse over the chorus. The verse identified the theme of the song, allowing the singer to ease into its mood.[10] In "Alexander's Ragtime Band," Berlin reduced the verse to sixteen bars and expanded the chorus to thirty-two. Berlin also changed keys between the verse and the chorus, which was seldom done.[11]

Just a few years later, another second-generation Jew wrote another influential song. Composed by the then relatively unknown George Gershwin, "Swanee," with the lyric by Irving Caesar, was first performed in 1919 in a revue called *Demi-Tasse*. The song, however, made no impression until Al Jolson interpolated it into *Sinbad*, his concurrently running show. Ironically, this theater-designed song of limited quality (at least compared to his later songs) became Gershwin's greatest hit. At the end of 1920, millions of copies of the sheet music had been sold, and it became a world-wide sensation.[12]

By this time musical revues such as *George White's Scandals* and *Earl Carroll's Vanities* were being staged, but it was the *Ziegfeld Follies* that had the longest run. While in Paris in 1906, Anna, the wife of Florenz Ziegfeld, suggested that he introduce to New York a musical variety show based on the French cabaret revue.[13] Back in

4

New York that year, Ziegfeld attended every show of the Broadway season and concluded that change was needed. What he observed was a standardized production in which about twenty young beauties (then called girls) went through three costume changes. The cast consisted of a leading lady, a straight man, dancers, and young lovers in a boy-meets-girl plot. Ziegfeld dispensed with the plot and overloaded the stage with beauty and magnificence—20 girls became 120 with as many as twenty changes. A dozen musicians was increased to 100. Six comedians were better than one.[14]

In 1907, on the roof of the New York Theatre renamed the Jardin de Paris, Ziegfeld presented his first revue, and from that date to 1943, but not always yearly, the *Follies* were staged at different theaters. Ziegfeld's success resulted from his ability to combine high and low culture. His chorus girls may have been dressed in the latest fashions, but his dancers performed the cakewalk, fox-trot, shimmy, and turkey trot. He would hire the classical composer Victor Herbert to write his scores but would introduce aspects of the ballet into musical-comedy sketches. Because the shows were basically a series of comedic routines and dance numbers, any song could be inserted anywhere.[15] Over the years, the *Follies* gave directors and choreographers opportunities to demonstrate their talents and songwriters an outlet for their compositions. The hits included "Shine on Harvest Moon"(1908), "By the Light of the Silvery Moon,"(1909), "Second Hand Rose,"(1921), "My Man,"(1921), and "Shaking the Blues Away," (1927).[16]

The golden age of the Ziegfeld revue began in 1915 when dance became an integral part of the show. Eight major dance numbers were introduced that included ballroom dancing, precision dancing, tap, ballet, and African-American jazz dancing. And in three vignettes, technology was a major theme. "Under the Sea" dealt with the invention of the submarine and "Radiumland" featured Radium girls. The revue also saw the introduction of German stagecraft by the architect and theatre designer Joseph Urban.[17] According to a theatre critic, the 1915 *Follies* was "a monster vaudeville pageant framed in plush, an organized comedy romp in a rose garden, a high-brow scenic revel shot with good low-brow fun."[18]

The thirteenth edition was staged at the New York's New Amsterdam Theatre in 1919. With songs by Irving Berlin and others, the show was directed and choreographed by Ned Wayburn, and the cast included Eddie Cantor, Marilyn Miller, and Bert Williams. Showgirls representing salads were featured in a production number. The Salvation Army was honored in the grand finale in which the topical number was "Prohibition" by Berlin. The stage was full of mourners, liquor lovers, and bartenders, and in a scene depicting a saloon of the future, chorus girls paraded as Coca-Cola, Sarsaparilla, grape juice, and lemonade. The revue also reflected how minstrelsy had influenced white musicals. In blackface, Eddie Cantor and Bert Williams (who was black) sang and discussed things in a standard semicircle minstrel format. Staged shortly after the end of the First World War when white audiences wanted escapist fare, the Follies of 1919 succeeded enormously. Berlin's "A Pretty Girl is Like a Melody" was the hit of the show.[19]

Beginning in 1923 Paul Whiteman, the so-called "King of Jazz," and his orchestra provided the music for the *Follies* for 333 performances.[20] Where Whiteman fits into the history of jazz, or even if he played jazz, has yet to be resolved by historians, musicians, and critics. But he was a well-educated musician who once played violin in the Denver Symphony, and he hired at one time or another the best talent available, including jazz greats Bix Beiderbecke, Frank Trumbauer, Eddie Lang, Bunny Berigan, and Joe Venuti. Their talents may have been under-utilized in Whiteman's very tight arrangements, but they were well paid and treated.[21] How well the orchestra supported the sketches and songs of the *Follies* is not known, but it could swing and its rhythm and beat must have affected the singers and dancers. That jazz-infused music was now influencing the musical theater seems evident.

In November, Whiteman attended a concert by soprano Eva Gauthier at New York's Aeolian Hall. The first important classical artist to add jazzy popular songs to her program, consisting of the works of Bartok, Bellini, Purcell, and Hindemith, she broke open the doors of the Hall for others to follow. With George Gershwin at the piano, she sang "Alexander's Ragtime Band," "The Siren's Song," "Leave It To Jane," "Carolina in the Morning," "I'll Build a Stairway to Paradise," "Innocent Ingenue Baby," and "Swanee." The audience went wild, compelling Gauthier to return for an encore, in which she sang Gershwin's "Do It Again." A reviewer wrote: "the six jazz numbers stood up amazingly well, not only as entertainment but as music. . . .They were not weighty, but neither is *Lauf der Welt*. They conveyed no profound message—but neither does a good deal of *Also Sprach Zarathustra*. . . .What they did possess was melodic interest and continuity, harmonic appropriateness, well-balanced, almost classically severe form, and subtle and fascinating rhythms—in short, the qualities that any sincere and interesting music possesses."[22]

Gauthier's success prompted Whiteman to present his own concert in the no longer hallowed territory of the Aeolian Hall. And he is perhaps best remembered for persuading Gershwin to compose "Rhapsody in Blue" and for introducing the composition at the Hall on February 12, 1924. Only one of eleven performances by a variety of composers, it was, with Gershwin at the piano, the hit of the concert. According to one critic, the middle section, "seemed to lag. But the beginning and ending of it were stunning. . . . With all its lag, diffuseness and syncopated reiterativeness, here was the day's most pressing contribution. Mr. Gershwin has an irrepressible pack of talents, and there is this element of inevitability about his piece." Another claimed "it was genuine jazz music, not only in its scoring but in its idiom. . . .Mr Gershwin will bear watching; he may yet bring jazz out of the kitchen."[23]

Although musicologists, historians, critics, and musicians have disagreed over the years regarding the quality of a solo, the importance of a particular style, and the significance of an arrangement, they all agree jazz was created by African Americans. Slaves introduced African music to North America wherever they were put ashore and began to chant or sing some kind of lament. When they first picked up and began to experiment with European musical instruments is impossible to know, although it was probably well after the first arrival. When jazz, as a distinct and self contained music, began also is difficult to pinpoint. As noted by classical composer and jazz historian Gunther Schuller, "Some historians use the year 1895 as a working date; others prefer 1917. . . .But whatever date is picked, it is safe to say that in purely musical terms the earliest jazz represents a primitive reduction of the complexity, richness, and perfection of its African and, for that matter, European antecedents."[24]

The music was born in New Orleans. Founded in 1718 by France, the city was ceded to Spain in 1764, only to return to France in 1800 which turned it over to the United States in 1803. A cosmopolitan city, European music and drama were regularly performed, and many of those in attendance were Creoles, the offspring of slaves and slave owners who gained their freedom long before the Emancipation Proclamation and who occupied a social position between whites and blacks. The first major theatre opened in 1792, followed by the Theatre d' Orleans in 1813. The American Theater opened in 1824 and the St. Charles Theatre the following year. The Varieties Theater was founded in 1848, the New Orleans Opera House in 1859. The latter was soon staging performances unrivaled in the western hemisphere. As noted by the historian Ted Gioia, "music of all types permeated New Orleans social life; whether high or low, imported or indigenous, it found a receptive audience in this cosmopolitan city. Has any city in history exhibited a greater love affair with the musical arts?"[25] Perhaps Vienna and Rome, but his point is well taken.

Although a slave city in a slave state, New Orleans exhibited more tolerance than most cities, a case in point being the City Council's decision in 1817 to establish an official site where slaves could dance on Sundays. The site became known as Congo Square. And in 1819, Benjamin Latrobe witnessed a gathering of five to six thousand slaves. The dancers were organized into four groups:

> In the first were two women dancing. They held
> each a coarse handkerchief extended by the corners
> in their hands, and set to each other in a miserably
> dull and slow figure, hardily moving their feet or

bodies. The music consisted of two drums and a stringed instrument. An old man sat astride of a Cylindrical drum about a foot in diameter, and beat it with incredible quickness with the edge of his hand and fingers. The other drum was an open staved thing held between the knees and beaten in the same manner. They made an incredible noise. The most curious instrument however was a stringed instrument which no doubt was imported from Africa. On the top of the finger board was the rude figure of a Man in a sitting posture, and two pegs behind him to which the strings were fastened. The body was a Calabash. It was played upon by a very little old man, apparently 80 or 90 Years old. . . .Most of the circles contained the same sort of dancers. . . .

A Man sung an uncouth song to the dancing which I suppose was in some African language, for it was not french [sic], and the Women screamed a detestable burthen on one single note. The allowed amusements of Sunday, have, it seems perpetuated here, those of Africa among its inhabitants.[26]

Obviously, Africans were perpetuating their culture through dance and music, but what the music sounded like is impossible to decipher. The basic rhythmic unit, however, may have been the eighth note, rather than the common European quarter-note division. As theorized by Schuller, the African "either thinks in eight notes, or, if he is momentarily thinking in quarter notes, is capable of feeling the eight-note subdivisions just as strongly at any given moment in his music."[27]

From this music evolved the blues which according to scholars combined the African pentatonic scale with the European diatonic scale. This resulted in the third and seventh intervals of the diatonic scale becoming known as "blue" notes. As explained by Ted Gioia, "This effect, which is impossible to notate, is one of the most gut-wrenching sounds in twentieth century music. Given its visceral impact, it is little cause for surprise that the device soon spread beyond the blues idiom into jazz and many other forms of popular music."[28]

Trumpeter Buddy Bolden, recognized as the first great jazz artist of the twentieth century, certainly played the blues but he never recorded. Moreover, had he been recorded, the New Orleans ensemble style he and others played during the first years of the century probably would sound today crude and certainly dated. But from this point, wrote Schuller, "jazz gradually developed not only in quality but also in basic conception and intent. The musicians who produced it were undergoing some very profound social changes, and their music obviously had to reflect this."[29] Those changes are exemplified in the half-a-million African Americans who migrated from the South to the North between 1916 and 1919. A million more left during the 1920s.

Paralleling the early development of jazz was ragtime. Essentially a music for the piano in which a syncopated melody is played over regularly accented rhythms, it emerged in the late nineteenth century. The music was designed to be played, not to be sung, and was written by African Americans. For a time, it was the music America danced to. Jazz scholar Winthrop Sargeant has written: "As it existed between 1905 and 1910 the rag offered the most intricate and interesting rhythmic development that has ever been recorded in our popular printed sheet-music. The rag writers of the early nineteen hundreds used every formula of syncopation, phrase distortion, and cyclical rhythmic structure that ingenuity could contrive. Polyrhythm flowered exuberantly. By 1909 every aspect of the three-over-four variety had been exploited, including complex superimpositions and exact repetitions of cyclical phrases. None of the sheet music industry's subsequent efforts have shown anything of comparable technical complexity."[30] Born about the same time as the musical, it is not surprising that rags would be incorporated into the revues, although the so-called rags by Irving Berlin and George M. Cohen were unimaginative in comparison to the real thing. As Thomas L. Riis has pointed out, "the coincident emergence of black music, especially ragtime, as a favorite form of popular music and 'musical comedy' as a distinctively American theater form stand out in bold relief."[31]

Black music and musical comedy clearly merged in *Shuffle Along,* written, produced, directed and performed by African Americans in 1921. A white critic found the music intoxicating: "At a grand piano in the orchestra pit sits Mr. Eubie Blake, composer of all the music. He is surrounded by fifteen helpful harmonists. Miss Lottie Gee or Roger Matthews comes down to the footlights and sets a metronomic foot to beating a rhythm. It travels down the expectant spine of Mr. Blake into his helpful fifteen's fingers [sic]. In two semi-quavers you are quivering to the same magic that has set all these spontaneous musicians to reeling melodiously. You may resist Beethoven and Jerome Kern, but you surrender completely to this."[32] The show may have introduced only aspects of jazz, such as syncopation, but the music reached a large audience, both white and black.

The jazz musicans who left New Orleans during the late teens and early twenties—individuals such as Freddy Keppard, Sidney Bechet, Jimmie Noone, King Oliver, Kid Ory, Johnny and Baby Dodds, and Louis Armstrong—introduced the real thing to the North. Also moving north were five white musicians who had formed the "Original Dixieland Jazz Band." After a stint in Chicago, the band moved to New York where in 1917 it recorded "Livery Stable Blues." That a white band playing the New Orleans ensemble style was the first to record music created by African-Americans has troubled some historians and critics, but it contributed to the spread of the music, which, in turn, benefited black musicians playing jazz. Obviously its members had learned the music from listening to African-Americans, but they also influenced those who listened to their records, such as Benny Goodman who was inspired by clarinetist Larry Shields.

"As a mainstream tradition, the New Orleans style in its pure early form did not survive the 1920's," noted Schuller. "Even King Oliver and Jelly Roll Morton succumbed to the pressures of changing styles, and their great recordings of that decade represent both the end of an era and the beginnings of a new one. A few orchestras stayed on in New Orleans and fought to maintain the pure style. They managed to survive economically to the end of the 1920s. But by then the inroads of the new solo style and influence of sweet and commercial bands had taken their toll, so that the large New Orleans-style ensemble had become a relic by 1930."[33]

Ironically, the recordings of those playing the early and later styles made permanent what in design was to be impermanent— the spontaneous moment of improvisation. By freezing in time that moment, however, the 78rpm phonographic record preserved what would have been lost forever. Without it, jazz might have remained little more than a strange kind of provincial music limited to New Orleans. The record not only preserved this music, it also determined the structure and length of songs. The performers had about three minutes to get their message across.[34]

Sheet music had long preceded the phonograph record as a means of transmitting music, but it was not a good medium for capturing the essence of jazz and the blues. The nuances of the music could not be notated, so it became largely a device for spreading popular songs. The publishers of sheet music and the producers of recordings competed for the same audience. Publishers sold more copies of sheet music than producers sold records, but the numerous record labels released many more songs than did the publishers. [35]

During the 1920s, the radio grew in popularity, and became an instrument crucial in the spread of jazz and other musical styles. As Susan J. Douglas has pointed out, "Possibly radio's most revolutionary influence on American culture and its people was the way it helped make music one of the most significant, meaningful, sought after, and defining elements of day-to-day-life, of generational identity, and of personal and public memory." The same could be said of the phonograph, but all kinds of music could be heard at any time of the day or night on the radio. Although classical music was broadcast, the poor fidelity of the first receivers often garbled the collective sound. Used to projecting their voices to the back of a theatre, sopranos found it especially difficult to curtail their volume in front of microphones. Much better suited to the radio was a soft, crooning approach first developed by Vaughn De Leath, "The First Lady of Radio," and later by Rudy Vallee and Bing Crosby. Moreover, the instruments favored by jazz musicians—the piano, clarinet and saxophone—transmitted a clearer sound on the radio than did violins, cellos, and oboes. The 2/4 and 4/4 rhythms made listening an exciting experience.[36]

Initially, songwriters were not enchanted with radio, but when the "American Society of Composers, Authors and Publishers" (ASCAP) persuaded Congress not to pass legislation that would allow radio stations to play copyrighted music without paying royalties to its members, they changed their minds. Tunesmiths then began to plug their songs over the air. During the 1920s, Chicago became the capital of radio broadcasting, its stations offering both opera and jazz. The first live radio broadcast by black jazz musicians may have been the duets of pianists Earl Hines and Lois Deppe on KDLA in 1921. As broadcasts presented the music of Bessie Smith, Louis Armstrong, Duke Ellington, Jelly Roll Morton, and others, jazz, thought by many blacks and whites to be lewd and lascivious, began to gain respectability.[37]

Douglas has astutely noted: "The coincidence of jazz and radio married an aural technology with the fruits of a primarily oral culture. It wasn't just the lyrics of Duke Ellington's 'Baby, Ain'tcha Satisfied?' or Louis Armstrong's 'Butter and Egg Man,' stimulated conversations about lost or promised love, referred to the great migration of blacks to the North, and conjured up the excitement and loneliness of city life. The music itself was full of information, and Armstrong especially displayed the vocal qualities of his instrument, the trumpet. In the oral culture of African Americans this music—including instrumental techniques that evoked speaking, crying, moaning, and laughing—conveyed histories large and small, and invested them with powerful emotions."[38] What was evolving, noted Artie Shaw, was a "living form of folk music, an idiom, a kind of music *in slang*."[39]

Louis Armstrong was already well known in New Orleans as an important cornet player when he was invited to join the King Oliver Creole Jazz Band in Chicago. As second cornetist to Oliver, he was supposed to be just another member of an ensemble. But in his recordings with Oliver, his technical facility emerged so strongly that, in the words of Gioia, it became "disturbingly subversive. Is it not a deliberate undermining of the collective aesthetic? Both in the flamboyance of his melody line, as well as in the power of his tone. . . ,Armstrong's work calls attention to itself. In the context of his later recordings, with their emphasis on solo paying, this magnetic quality is an asset, but in the setting of the Creole Jazz Band it disrupts the seamless blending of instrumental voices that is the crowning glory of the early New Orleans style."[40] If what Armstrong did with King Oliver was subversion, what he did on his own was revolution.

Because jazz had always been in a state of flux, the New Orleans style would have changed even without Armstrong, but certainly he gave it a jolt. In Chicago from 1925 to 1927, Armstrong recorded eighty-nine songs. With his wife Lil Harden on piano, Johnny Dodds on clarinet, Kid Ory on trombone, and Johnny St. Cyr on banjo, they recorded as The Hot Five. In 1927 Armstrong added Baby Dodds on drums and Pate Briggs on tuba to the group and formed the Hot Seven. By all accounts, these recordings changed jazz forever. Instead of playing within the ensemble as one of several voices, Armstrong played above it as the dominant voice. Most of the pieces lack composers' names attached to them, such as "Gut Bucket Blues," "Oriental Strut," "Muskrat Ramble," "Sunset Cafe Stomp," and "West End Blues" with its magnificent opening cadenza.[41] Only a few popular songs, such as "You Made Me Love You" and "I Can't Give you Anything but Love," were included.

After Armstrong changed *how* jazz should be played, he and others soon changed *what* would be played. As explained by Schuller, "It was as if pop music and commercial interests had been standing by in the wings, ready to move in on the fledgeling music. One by one major jazz artists—even those with a direct connection to the more integral, purer jazz materials evolved in New Orleans— succumbed to the influence of the thirty-two bar popular song and increasingly put them into their repertoires."[42]

In 1930 and 1931, Armstrong recorded popular songs such as "If I Could Be with You," "I Got Rhythm," "Rockin' Chair," "Star Dust," "All of Me," "Georgia on My Mind," "Lazy River" "I'm Confessin' and "I Love You," to name just a few.[43] And he also included songs from Broadway shows such as "On the Sunny Side of the Street," from the *International Revue* of 1930 and Fats Waller's "Ain't Misbehavin,'" from the all black revue *Hot Chocolates* of 1929. The latter is a perfect example of jazz and the musical theater intersecting. The music was performed by the Carrol Dickerson orchestra of Harlem, which included Armstrong.[44]

Clearly, African-Americans were the driving force in spreading New Orleans Jazz to Chicago and then to New York during the 1920s, but they were also some of the first to organize big bands, often called "territorial bands" because of their location in states such as Missouri. In 1923 Bennie Moten cut his first sides with a small group he had formed in Kansas City. The following year it consisted of eight musicians, and in 1926 it expanded to ten. Although the Moten band had few competitors during the remainder of the 1920s, several other black bands, especially those led by Alphonse Trent, Troy Floyd, and Walter Page, stand out. With the death of Moten in 1935, pianist Count Basie, formerly with Walter Page, took over the management of the band. It became his orchestra and lasted for decades.[45]

The contribution of the Moten band in the evolution of jazz is enormous. As pointed out by Schuller, the ten sides it cut in 1932 demonstrate "that hot swinging jazz need not be played loud. There are a dozen moments here where the band swings at low dynamic levels. The relaxation implied in this kind of controlled playing— control and relaxation are not incompatible—was possible only in relation to the rhythmic conception this magnificent rhythm section had evolved." A major part of the evolution was the replacement of the tuba with a string bass. On some songs, the 4/4 flow of the bass line would have been impossible on the tuba: "These recordings produced a rhythmic revolution comparable to Armstrong's earlier one. They spelled the doom of all earlier rhythm-section techniques."[46] The 4/4 bar emphasizes the weak beats. That is, in a 1, 2, 3, 4 bar, the 2 and 4 beats are stressed. Put another way, musicians will count one, two, three, four, but snap their fingers on two and four. This is the foundation for what is called "swing."

By 1932 jazz had "evolved aesthetic, stylistic, technical criteria which were to govern its future for some years without major changes or radical breakthroughs," noted Schuller. Those years extended to 1945 and have been labeled the "Swing Era," when jazz was America's popular music. "The language of jazz was veritably bursting at the seams, as creativity and technical innovation drove forward hand in hand. One need only listen to the music of Duke Ellington, Louis Armstrong, Jimmie Lunceford, the Moton/Basic bands and, later, some of white swing era bands to realize that jazz was literally exploding in myriad new directions— not only musically and stylistically, but geographically as well." No longer was jazz limited to a few cities. People could now hear it live in the numerous ballrooms that sprang up nationwide and on the radio and phonograph records.[47]

And the primary, but not the only, means of spreading this music was the big band, and it was no coincidence that the big band emerged during the Great Depression. According to Ted Gioia,

> a single band could now entertain countless listeners through the magic of radio. By implication, a few instrumentalists were doing the work that previously required hundreds, perhaps thousands of bands. Thus the same technology that brought unparalleled fame to a small cadre did irreparable damage to most players, as supply and demand were brought further out of alignment. Perhaps the growth of big bands during this era was as much a result of these economic forces as it was a sign of changing tastes. As wages declined and musician unemployment rose, a dozen players could be hired for relatively little. The big band, formerly a luxury, was now a standard format, as excess workers made labor-intensive activities—in music just as in production— more viable, hence more commonplace.[48]

The white bands have been categorized as either "sweet" or "swing." The former performed uncomplicated fox-trot arrangements for dinner-club audiences and were led by individuals such as Guy Lombardo, Eddie Duchin, and Hal Kemp. The swing bands also played at dances, but many of their arrangements were up-tempo with jazz rhythms. Charlie Barnet, Benny Goodman, and Artie Shaw fall into this category. Pianists, small groups, or combos as they were then called, and vocalists were also active, but it was the big band that defined the Swing Era. On records and in concerts and ballrooms, the bands made famous many theater and popular songs. They could do so, as Will Friedwald has pointed out, because "the classic American song is the most flexible form of music." Unlike most musical types, it can be played "in any tempo, in any time signature, in any style."[49] And it was during the Swing Era that tunesmiths produced some of their finest work. As a result, noted Schuller, "the American song is inextricably and profoundly linked with jazz, the one serving—along with the blues—as the basic melodic/harmonic material on which the other could build."[50]

Moreover, according to William and Nancy Young, arrangers also took advantage of the flexibility of the popular song to fit it to "the qualities of a particular orchestra or group, of giving an aggregation a singular sound. During the Swing Era, arrangers frequently emerged as important as song writers themselves."[51] For example, Fletcher Henderson, a leader of black swing band, ironically achieved recognition and financial success only after his arrangement of "King Porter's Stomp" was adopted and recorded by Benny Goodman. Fortunately, Henderson's importance in the era is now recognized.[52]

Big band leaders and arrangers were particularly drawn to Broadway songs, such as "Body and Soul," "But Not for Me," "Embraceable You," "Exactly Like You," "Love for Sale," "Alone Together," "Night and Day," "Don't Blame Me," "Just One of Those Things," "Have You Met Miss Jones?" "My Funny Valentine," and "Darn That Dream." And jazz musicians also recorded many songs written for the screen during the 1930s, such as "When Your Lover has Gone," "I Cover the Waterfront," "The Way You Look Tonight,"

"Some Day My Prince Will Come," "Love Is here to Stay," "A Foggy Day," and "Over the Rainbow." Thus, by the end of the decade, jazz and the songs of composers such as George Gershwin, Jerome Kern, Richard Rodgers, Irving Berlin, Cole Porter, Harold Arnold, Vincent Youmans, Arthur Schwartz, and Vernon Duke had become intimately linked.[53]

The most obvious example of a theater-composer's song becoming a jazz hit came in 1938 when Artie Shaw recorded Cole Porter's "Begin the Beguine," from the not very successful *Jubilee* of 1935. The recording sold more than two million copies and stimulated Shaw to record other show tunes. Ironically, Shaw and the record producers thought the other song on the record— "Indian Love Call"—had the best chance of success. Shaw wrote in his autobiography: "Who would have picked a tune to be a hit after the public had already heard it in a show and apparently been perfectly willing never to hear it again? How could anybody in his right mind figure to make a hit record out of a dead tune with a crazy title like *Begin the Beguine*?"[54]

That many of the songs by Jerome Kern, especially those he wrote for *Show Boat*, became hits is more understandable. Produced in 1927 by Florenz Ziegfeld, with the libretto and lyrics by Oscar Hammerstein II, *Show Boat* differed considerably from the musicals that came before it in that the plot and music were integrated. It contained the kind of elaborate scenery and costumes of the earlier plotless extravaganzas, but the story went in a new direction in that it dealt with miscegenation, and it did not end with its characters living happily ever after. Although the story may today seem "melodramatic and gauche," wrote Philip Furia, it was the first step in the integration of song and story.[55]

Of the several songs introduced, "Make Believe," "Bill," "Ol' Man River," and "Can't Help Lovin' Dat Man" became well known. As noted by Alec Wilder, elements of jazz can be found in "Can't Help Lovin' Dat Man." The "first, second, and fourth sections, all identical, were unusual for the time insofar as the notes of three quarters of each measure are based on a chord unrelated to the key in which the song is written and do have a resultant 'blue' tinge." Regarding "Ol' Man River," it is not a "complex song, melodically or harmonically. . . .Undoubtedly the lyric accounts for half of the song's acceptance,"[56]

In 1928 Bing Crosby and Paul Robeson each recorded "Ol' Man River" with the Paul Whiteman Orchestra. Robeson interpreted the lyric, Crosby sang it as a rhythm tune in an upbeat tempo. Crosby's version became a hit, Robeson's did not. But Robeson got some "revenge" when he sang it in the 1936 film of *Show Boat*. Frank Sinatra also performed the song in the 1946 film biography of Jerome Kern, *Till the Clouds Roll By*. Perched on a white pedestal in a white tux, backed up by a huge white-robed orchestra in all white art deco setting, and looking like a very white teenager, he sang a song about the misery of a black man in the South. This is a sight to behold and perhaps to treasure, if for all the wrong reasons.

After *Show Boat*, the integrated musical continued to evolve. Three political satirical musicals in the early 1930s—*Strike Up the Band* (first presented in 1927 but revised in 1930), *Of Thee I Sing,* and *Let' Em Eat Cake,*—advanced the process, but not until 1943, when Hammerstein teamed up with Richard Rodgers to create *Oklahoma*, was it completed. According to Ben Yagoda, in the integrated musical "The lyrics matured more quickly than the scripts; indeed, writing for Broadway elevated the work of lyricists as much as if not more than that of composers as the operetta style was replaced by more down-to-earth fare. The plots may not have been Shakespeare, but they were complemented by songs in a chest-voice vernacular, in contrast to the high-pitched heavy vibrato of yore. That vernacular touch meshed well with the wordplay, unexpected metaphors, and intricate rhyme schemes. . .with which the best lyricists began to do great things."[57]

To say, however, "that influx of successful 'adult' musicals sounded the knell of the song-and dance tradition would be erroneous," wrote a composer of both. "The 'song-and dancers' are as American as a hot dog and will be with us, in one shape or another, as long as the musical theater stays alive. Why shouldn't they? An expertly made 'song and dancer' is better entertainment by far than overly arty experiments, with or without a message."[58] Moreover, musical revues were the best place for composers and lyricists to publicize their songs. From them came many standards, the integrated musical producing far fewer hits. As observed by James T. Maher, "the most superficially charming *Follies*, blowzy *Scandals*, banal *Vanities*, or other similarly empty-headed serial entertainments, all good fun, have at times introduced well-written songs."[59]

Summing up the musical revolution that erupted in the United States, Tony Thomas has written:

> American music was undistinguished until the turn of the century. Stephen Foster had made an impression with his ballads, and people enjoyed the music of the minstrel shows, but very little of this music made an impact on the rest of the world. Slowly people in other countries became aware of spirituals and ragtime, and by the start of the First World War, the sound of blues began to insinuate itself. Here was a strange new quality in musical form, the very basis of jazz, a sound that quickly spread through the universe. . . .

> Suddenly a cluster of bright young men. . . . swamped Tin Pan Alley and Broadway with vital, tuneful songs that had a flavor and character recognizably American. All the influences seemed to meld at this time—the blues, the Negro themes, the ragtime, the folk music of multiple cultures brought by the immigrants, and the classical traditions and training of Europe.[60]

One of those European immigrants with classical training was from Russia. In a relatively short time he would compose several outstanding American songs.

Chapter Two
The Tunesmith:
From Vladimir to Vernon

On October 10, 1903, at a small railroad station in Parafianovo, Belarus, then part of the Russian Empire, Anna Alexeevna Dukelsky unexpectedly went into labor. The boy, Vladimir Dukelsky, born that day was technically speaking a native Russian, but as he noted in his autobiography:

> there is exactly one quarter of Russian blood in my veins. That was supplied by my mother's father, Alexis Kopylov, a self-made man of, I believe, peasant origin. He made his money in sugar, as he was general manager for the famous Count Bobrinsky Refineries. Kopylov married a pretty and rather social young girl who was half Viennese and half Spanish and whose name was von Köestel. On my father's side I am half Lithuanian and half Georgian (Caucasian); my grandfather, Vladimir Apollonvitch Dukelsky, was a highly placed official in Tiflis, where he occupied the post of general administrator under the Grand Duke Micheal, the lord lieutenant of Caucasus. Grandfather married the beauteous Georgian Princess Daria Toumanov, nicknamed Dariko and noted for her lavish parties, eccentricity of dress, and somewhat Catherine-the-Great-like self-assertiveness. Both grandmothers were extremely musical and played the piano quite well; the maternal one, according to the family legend, was Anton Rubinstein's favorite pupil and appeared in public playing her teacher's D-minor concerto with a provincial orchestra. . . .

Father and Mother were addicted to music in the customary manner of Russian dilettantes in comfortable circumstance. Father, a handsome man of medium height, with brilliant black hair and a resplendent mustache, was a civil engineer specializing in railroad building and occasionally given to singing gypsy songs in a pleasant baritone. Mother studied the piano diligently while an inmate of the Institute of Maidens of Gentle Birth (the equivalent of an American finishing school) in Kiev, and her two great passions, which I never shared, were Beethoven and Wagner.[1]

By eleven months Vladimir had acquired a smattering of Russian and French and had absorbed classical music literally under his mother's feet where she placed him while playing the piano. The music emanating from the gramophone, ranging from Italian operas to gypsy songs, also delighted him: "A ritual was established of lulling me to sleep each night with florid Italian airs." By the age of three, he was reading and writing, which startled no one, but when he began scribbling reams of meaningless poetry, which he recited to the uncomprehending butler and cook, his mother sent him to a psychiatrist: "He let me off easy, but recommended some more suitable sports and recreations (I was four at the time) rather than the pedantic pursuits in which I took such unreasonable pleasure."[2]

At the age of eleven he was admitted to the Kiev Conservatory. There, he met a "sad-eyed and long faced Vladimir Horowitz, who studied with Serge Tarnovsky and later with the celebrated Felix Blumenfeld; his piano playing was already dazzling, but most of us students championed Horowitz's friend and rival, Sasha Doubiansky, who tragically committed suicide in his early twenties. Horowitz specialized in Chopin and Liszt, whereas Doubiansky leaned toward the moderns, particularly the charming Polish composer Szymanovski, who later became my friend." In 1917 Vladimir joined Reinhold Glière's composition class that was also attended by newcomers who had fled the violence in St. Petersburg and Moscow with the outbreak of the Russian Revolution.[3]

The death of Vladimir's father in 1912 had left the family, which now included his brother Alexis, well off, and life remained fairly normal until they returned to Kiev from vacation. The central committee of the Workers and Soldiers Soviet and the Presidium of the Socialist-Democrat party, the Bolsheviks, had taken over the city. Large posters promised death to the enemies of the working class. As recalled by Vladimir:

> The lines outside the food shops lengthened daily. All clothing was severely rationed, shots rang out constantly, and the populace was asked not to leave home after sundown on certain evenings because of spreading disturbances. Alex and I were still handed our daily lunches carefully rapped by Mother and sent off to school, Alex to Naumenko's and I to the Conservatory, Mother warning us not to endanger ourselves in the crowded streets. Going to the opera or to concerts was now a perilous adventure as all bourgeois children and grownups were recognizable by their dress and manner and were automatically asked for their identification papers and often held for annoying and officious examinations.[4]

Despite the restrictions brought on by the revolution, Vladimir composed a four-movement string sextet in 1918, which along with some of his songs and piano pieces made up one half of a conservatory concert staged by Glière. By this time music had become "the one meager illusion of immortality in a rapidly vanishing world. I came down, in swift succession, with one disease after another, so that my health added to Mother's mounting tribulations; we were chronically undernourished and going into the country in search of food was now punishable by death." The political instability of the city obviously added to the family's problems, Kiev changing governments numerous times between 1917 and 1919. In December, Vladimir, Alexis, their mother, and

Colonel Alexis Fedorovitch Lvov, a family friend, boarded a train for Odessa.[5]

They took up residence in the palace of Vladimir's paternal uncle, Ilya Vladimirovitch Dukelsky, and Vladimir enrolled in the Odessa Conservatory where he studied counterpoint with Vitold Malishevsky. The palace was noted for its "celebrations," and at night was alive with women and music. When a balalaika orchestra was unavailable, Vladimir was called upon to play polkas, tangos, and "the increasingly popular American two-steps."[6] Thus, by the age of seventeen, Vladimir had become somewhat familiar with American popular music.

Soon he even dressed like an American. In Odessa at the time, Russia-born American soldiers were assisting the Red Cross. When they called for some English-speaking Russians to help guard the organization's warehouses, Vladimir volunteered, although his English was extremely limited. For his guard work he was promised space on a transport named the *Navaho* bound for Constantinople. He was given an Enfield rifle, which he had no idea how to handle, an American khaki uniform, and a Red Cross armband: "Our sentry duty passed uneventfully, except for handing a few prowling drunks over to the port police. At dawn we were served steaming coffee in big mugs and coarse black-bread sandwiches with country bacon; thus fortified, we were started off with a detailed itinerary of our 'round-up.' We must have been a strange sight—seven or eight undersized boys, dressed in American uniforms far too large for us, stepping along the deserted streets of the besieged city brandishing useless rifles." One of their duties was to pick up a middle-aged general who was dead drunk and furious when he learned what was in store for him. But he followed the young "soldiers," as did a fat colonel who "had to be forcibly parted from the blowzy mistress who was in bed with him. . . .None of the officers relished having to march, unshaven and unkempt, convoyed by scrawny youths."[7]

In 1919 Vladimir, his mother, brother Alexis, and Colonel Lvov boarded the *Navaho* that followed an old imperial navy ice-breaker out of the port in a snowstorm, and because of a dense fog it barely managed to reach the Bosporus Straits. "Death never seemed closer to any of us," Vladimir remembered. "A slight lurch—the ship shuddered, and suddenly glided forward as smoothly as if it were on the surface of a Swiss lake. 'We made it, we made it!' went up the cry, and most of us ran on deck to verify the miracle. We stood in the clear January air screaming our lungs out with joy—the blue Bosporus, soothing and serene, just as advertised."[8]

The Dukelskys found accommodations in Constantinople on the European side of the Bosporus which allowed Vladimir to pick up temporary jobs playing the piano in restaurants and in theaters showing silent films. He learned some popular songs such as "K-K-K-Katy" and "For Me and My Gal." Because "the Rose of Jazz, healthy and blooming, was by now firmly planted on the European shore of the Bosphorus," patrons at a salon called Mayak "began to request 'Hindustan,' 'Tell Me' and 'Till We Meet Again.' I promptly purchased all three, also Berlin's early successes and a thing mysteriously entitled 'Swanee' by a man improbably styled Geo. Gershwin. The Berlins were good in their way, but the Gershwin sent me into ecstasies. The bold sweep of the tune, his rhythmic freshness and especially, its syncopated gait, hit me hard and I became an 'early-jazz' fiend." He admitted, however, not being very fiendish for New Orleans Jazz, which he dismissed as "largely a collectively produced mood, anonymous and crude." If "Tea for Two," "The Man I Love,"and "Night and Day" were not jazz, so be it, but "you can have all the 'Tiger Rags' in the world." It was, therefore, not really jazz that inspired him but the jazz orientation and rhythmic inventiveness of Gershwin, Berlin, and others. He spent considerable time at the piano writing tunes in the American idiom, and even though his songs may have sounded American, he admitted that harmonically they were not.[9]

In 1921 the Dukelsky family sailed to New York. An American assistant to an official in the YMCA had secured for Alexis a scholarship at the Cushing Academy in Ashburnham, Massachusetts. Vladimir immediately found work in New York:

The catalogue of my would-be 'commercial' activities in the 1921-23 period denotes an uncommon versatility, if nothing else. I played accompaniments for ersatz gypsies in Second Avenue restaurants; wrote 'incidental' music for vaudeville performers, which they commissioned and then declined to buy, declaring it unsuitable; played piano on the stage for Alexander Oumansky's ballet vaudeville act on the Keith circuit; played piano for a small-time adagio team content with any old circuit as long as they got paid, which wasn't often; wrote music for Horace Goldin, the famed magician, who gave me two hundred dollars for labor involving a lullaby for a trick rabbit, a tango for vanishing handkerchiefs and suddenly appearing bouquets of roses, a languorous waltz for card tricks and a diabolic *galop* to denote the time-honored feat of sawing a woman in half; conducted an orchestra of five musicians for a burlesque show, an exploit that deserves little digression.[10]

Vladimir was also taking the first tentative steps toward becoming a tunesmith. Once the Dukelskys had settled in Washington Heights, he would take the subway to the heart of the city to wander around Tin Pan Alley. He managed to get a hearing now and then, but his songs, not being in the idiom of the street, were rejected. He admitted that his melodies were not very good, and relying on a Russian-English dictionary, his lyrics even worse. In a song called "Spooning on a Crowded Bus," he came up with "Underneath the bridge our paradise we *cross*, spooning on a crowded *bus*." Not surprising, the song was rejected, as was "Don't Waste Your Time Wasting Your Time on Me." [11]

Dukelsky continued to compose classical music, but later realized that he had been leading a duel musical existence: "I began to torture and complicate the musical dialectics in my 'serious' output; thus, the simpler and more down-to-earth my tunes, the more cerebral and *voulu* my 'good' music became, until it was practically indistinguishable from that of the twelve-tone boys." But two of his ten songs on avant garde Russian poems were performed at program sponsored by the International Composers Guild. George Gershwin, whose song "Swanee" had so impressed him in Constantinople, was in the audience and later told him he was surprised that someone so young could write such dry intellectual stuff. Gershwin was greatly impressed with Vladimir's musical background, but what was he going to do with it he asked on another occasion. Vladimir's response was to play a cerebral piano sonata. There was no money or heart in that kind of stuff, said George. Don't be scared of going lowbrow. Write some popular tunes. They will open you up. In his autobiography, Vladimir wrote: "That rather startling remark of George's—'they will open you up'—stayed with me through all the years that we were friends." Later, Vladimir played some "freshly written tunes" for George, who shrugged off the first two, but the third so impressed him that he decided to take the young composer to meet Max Dreyfus, the publisher of Harms, Inc. In the waiting room were notable musicians, composers and lyricist in the employ of Dreyfus, such as Vincent Youmans and Oscar Levant. To George's surprise, Dreyfus did not like the song.[12]

Vladimir became increasingly dubious he had a future in music, popular or classical. In 1923 he wrote a piano concerto he played at parties but only after George had stunned the audience with "Do it Again" and "Stairway to Paradise." Arthur Rubinstein was very impressed with the composition and encouraged Vladimir to go to Paris, then the Mecca of young composers.[13] He took the advice but needed money. He turned to Gershwin for help:

> It transpired that George overburdened with work, needed a 'ghost' writer for a black-and-white ballet— a simple bit of ragtime for a high-kicking precision routine—for the Tiller girls, who were to appear in the 1924 edition of George White's *Scandals*. I turned out the thing in a few hours and was paid $100 by George. Deeming the job satisfactory, George then desired to have me try my hand at 'piano copies,'

publishable voice and piano versions of songs to be used in the revue. I arranged six of these and was paid twenty dollars apiece by Harms, Inc. The songs I 'arranged' were the ever-popular 'Somebody Loves Me,' 'In Araby,' 'Kongo Kate,' 'Tune in on Station J-O-Y,' 'Year After Year,' and a rhythm song, the name of which escapes me. I was quite proud of the 'fill-ins,' I provided for 'Somebody Loves Me' and was amused to find that they were also used in the stock orchestration—obviously, the arranger thought them eminently Gershwinesque, which indeed they were. That was another $120.[14]

Max Dryfus also hired him to write a solo piano arrangement for "Rhapsody in Blue." Before sailing he wrote to George, noting he was having difficulty with the arrangement and had been "rather restless lately, thanks to visas, passports and other junk."[15] But with an additional $500 he got for playing at the house of a prominent Bostonian, he had accumulated $800, more than enough for a six months sojourn in Paris.[16]

If Vladimir had any doubts about leaving New York for Paris, they were soon put to rest. Quickly, the musical elite of the city—in particular Sergei Prokofiev and Serge Pavlovitch Diaghilev—recognized him as a promising young composer. Thus, he could not believe his luck when Diaghilev, Russian art critic, patron and ballet impresario, commissioned him to compose a ballet based on the legend of Zephyr and Flora. On August 4, 1924 he wrote to Gershwin, then in London, about his good fortune, noting that his ballet was to be produced for the eighteenth season of the Ballet Russes: "Of course, you understand that nothing better could have happened to me, and, although speed is not required in this particular case, I'm writing and writing. In two weeks I'm going to Monte Carlo to join Diaghilev, finish the score and start rehearsals." He also told George that he had spoken to Diaghilev about him "and played nearly all your tunes to his secretary, who finds them amazing. . . .Do come to Paris before I leave."[17] From Monte Carlo, he sent a postcard to George: "my ballet is progressing steadily. I already wrote the overture, and three numbers. Diaghileff [sic] is quite satisfied. . . .Do write all about yourself."[18]

Zephyr and Flora premiered in Paris on June 15, 1925 to critical acclaim. One reviewer wrote: "A musician like Dukelsky, armed with an excellent technique, discovers in one fell swoop a liberated style for which we, in our country, are searching in vain. The score of 'Zephire' offers a richness and an abundance of rhythms and a savor of sounds that make it a perpetual treat for the ear." Another critic thought that the score was "a copious work, filled, I would almost say *stuffed* with music, which reveals qualities of the first order." Even though the composer did not yet know how to curb his language, "can you think of a more praiseworthy defect? So many composers have nothing to choose from, since they have nothing to say!" The debut contained "more than merely promises and Mr. Dukelsky can be proud of a most merited success." The Paris *Herald Tribune* enthused: "This score, so new and so alive, seems to me, next to the gigantic production of Stravinsky's, one of the most significant works of modern music, and Russian music in particular."[19]

While in Paris, Vladimir met the Russian music critic and musicologist Igor Glebov who knew about his friendship with George Gershwin, a legendary figure even in Russia. Glebov proposed that he translate some of the librettos and lyrics from Gershwin shows, in particular those from *Lady Be Good* and *Funny Face:* "So uncommon a proposition greatly intrigued me, as I felt that no better anti-Soviet propaganda could be imagined than a big, healthy dose of Gershwin music,

Vladimir Dukelsky in Monte Carlo, 1924,
Vernon Duke, Passport to Paris

29

and all the good American things it stands for. That night after dinner I tinkered with 'Fascinating Rhythm' and 'Lady Be Good,' succeeding in Russianizing them quite expertly." Glebov took the lyrics and piano copies to Russia, but Vladimir never heard from him again.[20]

During the remainder of the 1920s, Vladimir and Diaghilev spent considerable time in London. And shortly after arriving on their first visit to produce *Zephyr and Flora*, he and Diaghilev met the English critic Edwin Evans in the Savoy Hotel. Vladimir gave "the bearded sage" a colorful account of his beginnings and confessed that his "love for jazz was never platonic, due to my friendship with George Gershwin." Asked about his ideas on music, Vladimir "made a few reasonably snappy remarks," noting that he hated all modernism but loved being modern. He believed in construction only in the truly classical sense, claiming it was more difficult to construct a fox trot than to write, as the modernists do, a thousand poems on golden fishes, bald Chinamen, or oyster shells. He noted that jazz was "classicism for minors" and thus very useful.[21] Obviously, Vladimir had not been cured of the jazz bug, or at least that insect he called jazz.

Once *Zephyr and Flora* was performed, he signed a contract with a publishing firm that insisted he could only use his name for his "highbrow" music. Therefore, he took George Gershwin's advice and adopted "Vernon Duke" for his "lowbrow" music. "Try a Little Kiss," his first published song as a tunesmith, was interpolated into *Katja, the Dancer*, at Daly's Theater in the West End. Jimmy White, the producer, had contracted Duke to "pep up" the show, then in its second year, with some of "that bloody Yankee monkey music." To Vernon it was "a mystery that White should have applied to me, a Parisian Russian, according to the London press, for Yankee monkey music, but he handed me a very welcome contract and I started a career of 'doctoring' ailing Viennese operettas and 'jazzing 'em up' to suit the changing tastes of Daly's audience."[22] He also wrote several songs for *Yvonne*, a revue with a libretto he called "inane." The lyricist found his "American-style tunes rather difficult to lyricize," but Vernon wrote several numbers he thought were "mildly pleasant, comfortably Kern-like in spots."[23]   In a letter to George, he mentioned that the show had run for thirty-four weeks and that he had sold ten songs to different managers. He now wrote all his lyrics which was "great fun." London was dreary, the parties boring.[24] In 1928 he composed his first entire score for *Yellow Mask,* which received a good notice from the *Daily Mail* and a congratulatory letter from Gershwin.[25]

Freed from this undertaking, he returned to Paris where George, brother Ira and his wife Leonore, and their sister Francis had checked into Hotel Majestic. The visit Vernon paid them in April did not go well. As recorded by Ira, George told Duke about a party hosted the previous night by the Polish-French composer Alexandre Tansman. George sought Duke's views on several composers including Tansman. Duke considered him a second-rater, but Vittorio Rietie was very good; E. Robert Schmitz was also very good; but Jacques Ibert was second rate. George then listed a few more, "Duke sniffing all the while. Then he said, 'You shouldn't have gone to that party. It will hurt you, people like that.'" Duke also got into an argument with George over parts of "An American In Paris," claiming he had allowed himself to become saccharine. When Duke left, the English composer Sir William Walton, a friend of both George and Vernon, advised George to disregard Duke's remarks, because he was under the spell of Prokofiev and considered anyone who wrote in any other style old fashioned.[26]

On June 14, 1928, Duke attended the premier of his First Symphony, conducted by Serge Kouissevitsky. Also on the program were fragments of Prokofiev's opera *Fiery Angel.* Vernon thought his work held up well against the master's. For a year business and pleasure took him to Berlin, back to Paris and then to London, where he concluded his future would best be served elsewhere. He sold about a dozen songs to a producer of a show that became, *Open Your Eyes,* settled a few debts, got a visitor's visa, paid a fraction of the British taxes he owed, and on June 22, 1929 boarded the *Laconia* "with the firm intention of giving America a second chance to discover me."[27]

Apparently the rift with George Gershwin did not last, because once he settled in Boston he asked him for a loan of $120, which he promised to repay in a month. George was not to mention his request to anyone and to send the money immediately, if he was so inclined.[28] When the money arrived, Vernon thanked George profusely: "You have already done so much for me that I only hope to be able to repay you one day for your true friendship, which I value more than anybody else's."[29] A short time later, he asked George to contact Max Dreyfus, who had hired him to write some songs, about his contract that had not arrived. Until it came, he could not afford to live in New York.[30] And still later, he requested another $150, promising to repay him "as promptly as the sum I borrowed last time." If George agreed, he was to make out the check to Vernon Duke.[31]

In late 1929 or early 1930, Vernon wrote to Gershwin about finishing the orchestration of his Second Symphony and about writing a double bass concerto.[32] In February 1930, Duke's piano sonata was performed at a concert produced by Aaron Copland and Roger Sessions, and the Boston Flute Players' Club presented his "Canzonetta," written for flute, oboe, viola, French horn, bass clarinet and bassoon.[33]

Duke wrote to Gershwin in April, noting that the third rehearsal of the Second Symphony was proceeding and that the first moment was "very satisfactory." The coda was "taken twice too fast," but it would be corrected at the next and final rehearsal. He was dying for George's opinion of the work [34] Duke admitted in his autobiography that he was "apprehensive about the symphony's Boston fate, owing to my inability to make suggestions or last-minute alterations in the score. For once my fears were groundless; Koussevitzky straightened out the sore spots or glossed them over and the symphony scored an emphatic success."[35]

About this time, Duke began a relationship with Paramount Publix, which had studios in Astoria, Long Island: "I was given a freshly scrubbed cubbyhole of an office, with my name in modest-size letters on he door, a tinny upright, a writing desk, a music cabinet and a telephone, and told to write whatever music

Paramount needed. I enjoyed turning out a song with [E.Y.] Harburg for a two-reel short in the morning and a few pages of 'emotional' background music for a dramatic feature in the afternoon." Because the music cabinet contained hundreds of stock arrangements, all he had to do was pull out of the drawers labeled "Anger," "Hysteria," "Seduction," "Passion," or "Religion" and select something that fit the particular scene he was assigned to. The picture he most enjoyed working on was *Laughter*, in which Fredrick March played a romantic composer: "During one scene he was required to play a three-minute 'rhapsody' (composed by me) on the piano; I also performed this piece in the film, with March going manfully through the correct pianistics—in this I had to coach him." Soon Vernon was earning ninety dollars a week, and when not scoring for Paramount was lent to other companies, such as Warner Brothers, to "'musicalize' trailers, those idiotic few-minutes previews of a coming attraction."[36]

Parallel with his Paramount engagement was his introduction to Broadway. At a party at the Gershwins, he played "I Am Only Human After All." Present was Theresa Helburn, one of the founders of the Theater Guild. She encouraged him to audition the song and others for the Guild's production of the third (1930) edition of *Garrick Gaieties*. The first two editions had launched the careers of Richard Rodgers and Lorenz Hart. Although one of several tunesmiths who got their songs accepted, Duke managed to convince the producers that five of his were worthy of inclusion, including "Too, Too, Divine" from *Open Your Eyes*, "Shavian Shivers," and "I Am Only Human After All." With a lyric by Ira Gershwin and E. Y. Harburg, the latter was published by Harms and received a positive review in *The New Yorker*. The revue had a four-months' run in New York. For its out-of-town tour Duke and Harburg wrote five more songs including the critics favorites "Unaccustomed as I Am" and "A Little Privacy."[37] In 1930 the Colonial Club Orchestra, the Arden and Ohman Orchestra, and Joe Vinuti and his New Yorkers recorded "I am Only Human After All." I suspect Duke favored the latter, Vinuti being a jazz violinist.

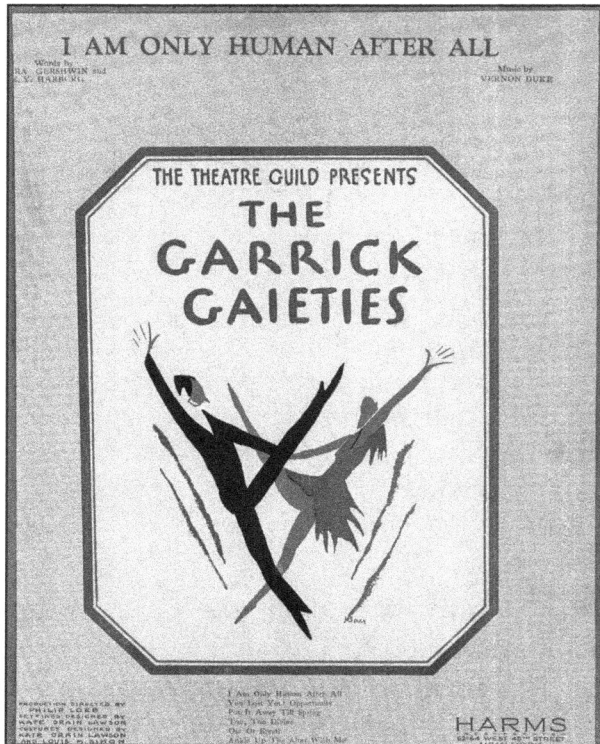

Sheet Music for the Garrick Gaieties

His visitor visa having expired, Duke sailed for Mexico in May 1931, needing a foreign country to obtain a quota number and from where he could reenter the U.S. as an immigrant and become eligible for citizenship. He loved Mexico City, but when his quota number was obtained he returned to New York, where he "could have kissed the 'sidewalks of New York,' so great was my joy at walking them again, and even thought of writing a modern version of the affecting old ballad." Soon after his arrival, impresario Billy Rose hired him at fifty dollars a week to review all the manuscripts that poured in for a revue to be called *Corned Beef and Roses*. The show never opened which may have been for the best.[38]

In April 1932, while having drinks at Tony Soma's famous establishment known as "West Side Tony's, with, among others, Dorothy Parker, Robert Benchley, and Monty Woolley, someone cried out "Oh to be in Paris now that April's here!" Vernon thought there was a great title for a song in that phrase, and the party repaired to a piano upstairs where he wrote "April in Paris." Tongue-in-cheek Duke recalled that he had "just given birth to a masterpiece that was certain to 'make the show.'"[39]

E. Y. Harburg, who had never been to Paris, wrote the lyric after reading travel brochures of the city, and the song was added to the revue *Walk a Little Faster*. With a libretto by S. J. Perelman, lyrics by Harburg, and music by Duke, the show, after a tryout in Boston, opened in New York on December 7, 1932 and ran for 119 performances. Late in his life, Harburg recounted his collaboration with Duke:

> I liked Vernon's facility. He was fast and very sophisticated, almost too sophisticated for Broadway. *Walk a Little Faster* had some very smart stuff in it. In fact, that's when I bounced out of the bread-and-butter stage into sophistication. My light-verse background popped up to reinforce me, and I could write much easier with Vernon than I could with some of the others. It was light, and airy, and very smart.
>
> Vernon brought with him all of that Noel Coward/Diaghilev/Paris/Russia background. He was a global guy with an ability to articulate the English language that was very interesting. A whole new world for me. He could drive you crazy, and he could also open up a new vista. Maybe it was a little bit chi-chi and decorative, but with my pumpernickel background and his orchid tunes we made a wonderful marriage. Maybe we were a strange mixture. We didn't compromise with each other. I applied the everyday down-deep things that concerned humanity to his sense of style and grace, and I think it gave our songs an almost classic feeling, along with some humor. We came together at a certain point, and for a while it was fine. He

satisfied my sense of light verse and the need for sophistication.[40]

A Boston critic raved about the revue: "Modernisms abound in Mr. Duke's music. He has confided it and Mr. [Conrad] Slinger has scored it. . .for a jazz, rather than a theater orchestra. Being a modernist, Mr. Duke makes bold rhythms. . . . Nor does Mr. Duke hesitate at modulations that might grate on the more innocent Berlin or Kern. Yet when need is, he can write a nostalgic, quasi-sentimental melody. . . .'April in Paris' is worthy, in place and kind, of that city in the spring."[41] Biographer Isaac Goldberg told Vernon that he thought the song was one of the finest compositions that had ever graced an American musical. If he had his way, he would make a study of it compulsory in all harmony courses.[42] Music critic Samuel Steatton noted "'April in Paris,' a song from one of the last season's revues has been called one of the finest light songs to have been sung on our stage during the past ten years. This particular Vernon Duke chanson is mentioned because it revealed the hitherto unknown possibilities of a supposedly overworked form and turned it into a frame full of resiliency and verve. It is the ability of Duke to 'revert' to Dukelsky when writing popular tunes that results in middle sections that are as catchy and appealing as the usual eight bar stroke of genius that is characteristic of the Tin Pan Alley school."[43]

In January 1933, Goldberg wrote an article for the *New York Evening Post*, entitled "Dukelsky into Duke." He considered "it important for our lighter musical stage that talent such as Duke's should not, at this point in his development, pass insufficiently appreciated. The man has an individual gift that makes him stand out in company of those who have made of our musical comedy something more than the dull routine it once used to be. . . .[I]f he is not allowed to find his place in contemporary revues, musical comedies and even comic opera, the loss will be, to us and to him, artistically considerable."[44]

The greatest praise for his music came while waiting in the publishing offices of Max Dreyfus. There, Duke encountered "a white-haired, bird-like little fellow who said in high-pitched voice: 'You're Vernon Duke, aren't you: Let me shake your hand —I'm Jerome Kern.' We shook hands and I murmured something indicative of my profound respect for the dean of America's show composers, who interrupted me to say: 'You may think it odd and I'm not in the habit of saying such things, but I'm crazy about your music—it's new and it's fresh. Believe it or not, I'm under your influence. Good day to you.'"[45]

In May 1933, producer Lee Shubert asked Vernon to assist him with the score for a new edition of the *Ziegfeld Follies*. Bobby Connolly was to direct, Fanny Brice to star. "Most revues," wrote Vernon, "are disorganized in the early stages, before the unnecessary material gets weeded out and the whole vehicle starts taking shape, but in the *Follies of 1933-34* sheer chaos reigned triumphantly. After weeks of quarrels, tantrums, firing, hirings, Connolly's disappearances, Lee Shubert's dreaded entrances, money and tears flowing, stagehands fleeing, we got off to an unpromising start in Boston. . . .True Fanny stopped the show, as was her habit, but faulty cues and backstage mishaps stopped it too—often. We expected a real lambasting from the critics, but to everyone's surprise they loved the show."[46] After engagements in Philadelphia, Washington, Pittsburgh, and Newark, the show opened on January 4,1934 in the Winter Garden in New York City. It is best remembered as the venue in which Fanny Brice introduced her "Baby Snooks" character. It ran for 182 performances and proved profitable for its producers.[47]

From the show came "I Like the Likes of You, " with the lyric by Harburg. It is a rhythm song par excellence, one in which the melody and harmony allow musicians to swing it. In *America Popular Song,* Alec Wilder noted that it "is alive and undated (in terms of professional writing) as any great song should be." "What Is There to Say?," was also praised by Wilder. He called it "one more great model of theater song writing. Again it's a case of every note counting and not one false move along the way." He was especially impressed with the four sets of quarter note triplets in the second phrase of the chorus.[48] And Harburg's lyric about the confusion of love ends in a way that shatters the canon of the popular love song: "My head is in a deadlock, I'd even face wedlock with you."

For the revue, Duke also wrote "Water Under the Bridge," a song he later described as "the first of the 'out of this world' (not heavenly, just plain uncommercial) tunes for which I achieved considerable notoriety; I don't want to call myself a prophet, but the odd harmonic structure of the piece, written in 1933, has all the earmarks of postwar 'bop' [jazz] conceptions." Duke could not get the song published, but in 1934 he recorded it with vocalist Bonnie Lake and clarinetist Ralph McLane. "I'm Mad About a Man About Town," with his own lyric, is on the reverse side of the record. This is the first recording by Duke of any of his works.[49]

That year, a future standard emerged from his fertile mind. He wrote both the music and the lyric to "Autumn in New York" that was interpolated into the revue *Thumbs Up!*[50] To Alec Wilder, "The verse may be the most ambitious I've ever seen. It begins simply enough, but halfway through it's almost as if the other musical half of the man couldn't be silent and the rest of the verse was finished by Dukelsky. It is extremely difficult and very lush." Wilder approved of its "experimental nature."[51]

The verse ends with "So on this gray & melancholy day / I'll move to a Manhattan Hotel / I'll dispense with my rose-colored chattels / And prepare for my share of adventures & battles / Here on the twenty-seventh floor / Looking down at the city I hate & adore." The lyric of the chorus offers "Glittering crowds & shimmering clouds In canyons of steel / They'er making me feel—I'm home / It's autumn in New York." And "Oh, autumn in New York / It lifts you up when you run down / Yes, jaded roués and gay divorcees / Who lunch at the Ritz / Will tell you its divine." Philip Furia has observed that rhymes such as "glittering crowds and shimming clouds" and "jaded roués and gay divorcees," give "the lyric a jaunty urbanity" that clashes with Duke's "efforts to create a melancholy mood of joy."[52] Unlike "April in Paris" which became an instant hit, "Autumn in New York" took longer, mainly because its complex verse and lengthy chorus are difficult to sing. Strangely, Duke barely mentioned "Autumn in New York" in his autobiography, whereas "April in Paris" received several paragraphs.

By 1934 Vernon Duke had become well-known as a composer of classical as well as popular music. Because of his "dual personality," he was labeled, perhaps first by Elizabeth Borton, the "Jekyll and Hyde" of music. But he told her "The two idioms which I write are as different as work and play. Jazz is easy for me—that is just recreation for which I happen to get paid." And paid well, added Borton, "for he has had success on Broadway in more shows than one—the latest being the Ziegfeld Follies of this year." Duke was equally frank when he admitted "If somebody commissioned me to write a song praising American buckwheat, and offered me money for it, I would write it. The greatest musicians and artists, after all, earned their living by what they did. They were so resourceful that they could turn any chance necessity into a living art." With Duke, resourcefulness extended beyond music. Borton noted that he was a Stage Door Johnny, who can often be found "sitting in the wings during rehearsals, keeping time occasionally with his cane. . . and dropping an attentive eye toward every shapely ankle on its way by."[53]

Music critic James B. Reston wrote in September 1935 that of all the "characters on Broadway, none seems more interesting than Vernon Duke of that particular quarter of the street known as Tin Pan Alley. He is the Sir Arthur Sullivan of the Rialto, and true Dr. Jekyll and Mr. Hyde. . . .Duke is Duke only when he writes popular music, which he is now doing for the new version of the Ziegfeld Follies. The rest of the time, he is Vladimir Dukelsky, and under this name he writes lofty symphonic pieces. There are some who predict a great future for him in the latter field, but most of the critics are inclined to believe his April in Paris will outlast the more erudite numbers."[54]

"April in Paris" would become a standard and outlast some of his "erudite numbers." But with the help of a famous lyricist so would another song he wrote a short time later.

Chapter Three
The Lyricist:
From Israel to Arthur to Ira

In 1891 Moishe Geshovits and Rosa Brushkin arrived separately in New York. Jewish immigrants from St. Petersburg, Russia where they had met, they quickly became Morris Gershvin and Rose Bruskin. At the time, a name change was thought to advance the Americanization process. Changing Gershvin to Gershwin would come later. On July 21,1895 they were married in an Eastside restaurant, the wedding festival apparently lasting three days. Israel (later known as Ira) entered the world on December 6, 1896. Jacob (later known as George) was born on September 28, 1898, Arthur on March 14, 1900, and Frances on December 6, 1906.[1]

The offspring were subjected to a father who was suspicious of banks, who pawned their mother's diamond ring when cash was needed, and who paid only cursory attention to their religious upbringing, Israel being the only child to have a bar mitzvah. By changing occupations on numerous occasions, Morris guaranteed that the family remained financially insecure. He operated or owned bakeries, a restaurant, Russian and Turkish baths, a hotel, a cigar store, a pool hall, a rooming house, and a bookmaking establishment. Morris insisted on living close to where he worked, so the family was in constant flux. By 1906, the Gershvins had lived in twenty-five buildings in Manhattan and three in Brooklyn.[2]

At their Second Avenue apartment in Manhattan, an event occurred in 1910 that would dramatically change the life of the Gershvin family—the delivery of an upright piano. Hoisted up the side of the apartment building where they lived and eased through a window, the piano was bought for Ira, but it had barely touched the floor when George, then twelve years old, began playing a popular tune. As recalled by Ira, "I remember being particularly impressed by his left hand. I had no idea he could play and found out that despite his roller skating activities, the kid parties he attended, the many street games he participated in (with an occasional resultant bloody nose) he had found time to experiment on a player-piano at the home of a friend on Seventh Street."[3] George's usurpation did not bother Ira who was much more interested in books than music, which he never learned to read.[4]

As a lifelong friend of the Gershvins recalled, the brothers possessed vastly different personalities: "If George was streamlined and propulsive, Ira was reserved and scholarly. He was gently humorous. One sensed in Ira even at the very center of involvement, a well of detachment. George gave you everything at once; he was boyish, with an extraordinarily sweet character. He wanted his listeners to participate in the excitement of his own development."[5] Whereas Ira seems in no hurry to find a career, George immediately embraced song writing. He quit school at age fifteen to plug songs on Tin Pan Alley, and published his first song in 1916. He also changed the spelling of his name to "Gershwin," as did the entire family.[6]

The high school attended by Ira stressed training in classical poetic forms, and he became passionate about light verse. Ira and his friend and future lyricist E. Y. (Yip) Harburg satirized their teachers and classmates in quatrains while in high school and wrote light verses at City College of New York in a column called "Gargoyle Gargles." But finding college, especially mathematic courses, not to his liking, Ira dropped out to work in his father's bathhouse. Now and then he managed to get a poem published in newspapers, but rejections were the rule. He did benefit, however, from the advice of Paul M. Potter, an English playwright who lived above the bathhouse. After reading Ira's "The Shrine," a satirical sketch, he told him to forget about that kind of writing and learn American slang. He should listen and observe as well. He also recommended that he send "The Shrine," to *The Smart Set*, edited by H. L. Mencken and George Jean Nathan. On November 14, 1917, Ira received a check for only one dollar, but at least it was from H.L. Mencken.[7]

With time on his hands, Ira often walked the streets of New York, taking in the cacophony of sounds. One entry in his diary reads: "Heard in a day: An elevator's purr, a telephone's ring, telephone's buzz, a baby's moans, a shout of delight, a screech from a 'flat wheel,' hoarse honks, a hoarse voice, a tinkle, a match scratch on sandpaper, a deep resounding boom of dynamiting in the impending subway, iron hooks on the gutter."[8] Throughout his career, Ira sought to capture in his lyrics the sounds and activities of everyday life. According to Deena Rosenberg, "An unusually large proportion of the cleverest light versifiers and humorists were children of east European immigrant Jews. . . .They yearned to be part of the American world, and the traditional Jewish emphasis on literacy and verbalization led to an eager master of the current idiom—colloquialisms, puns, double-entendres, word-play, and slang included. This was their language, not their parents', and they mastered it completely."[9]

Through the assistance of his brother George, Ira got a part-time job at the *New York Clipper*, a trade newspaper, where he wrote occasional reviews of vaudeville shows. He also wrote "The Great American Folk Song (Is a Rag)." After several revisions of the lyric, he showed it to George who dashed off a melody. The lyric, however, did not fit the melody. After more revisions including a name change to "The Real American Folk Song," it was interpolated into the musical *Ladies First*. But when it failed to impress audiences, the producer insisted on more changes. Ira refused and it was eliminated from the show. Terribly upset over the issue, Ira considered dropping lyric-writing completely, but his younger brother changed his mind.[10]

Early in 1920 George was commissioned to write a song for the star of *The Sweetheart Shop*. George asked Ira to write the lyric which he did under the nom de plume Arthur Francis, the names of his brother and sister. "Waiting for the Sun to Come Out," was accepted, interpolated, and published. Although the show lost money, its producer invited George and Ira to write the songs for *A Dangerous Maid*. The show closed in its out-of-town tryout in Pittsburgh in 1921, but one of the songs—"Boy Wanted"—was good enough to later be used in another play. Clearly, Ira had arrived as a legitimate lyricist, and between 1921 and 1924 he collaborated with composers other than his brother. Most of the songs were interpolated in shows already in existence. In 1924 he joined George S. Kaufman and Marc Connelly in the production of *Be Yourself.* Not a smash hit by any means, but the program stated that Ira Gershwin—not Arthur Francis—wrote the lyrics.[11]

Beginning in 1924, Ira worked almost exclusively with his brother, their first venture being *Lady, Be Good*, and a good one it was, producing "Oh! Lady, Be Good!," "Fascinating Rhythm," and "The Man I Love." Regarding the latter, Ira recalled its genesis: "In the spring of 1924 when I finished the lyric to the body of a song—the words and tune of which I now cannot recall—a verse was in order. My brother composed a possibility we both liked, but I never got around to writing it up as a verse. It was a definite and insistent melody—so much so that we soon felt it wasn't light and introductory enough, as it tended to overshadow the refrain and demand individual attention. So this overweighty strain, not quite in tune as a verse, was, with slight modification, upped in importance to the status of a refrain. I gave it a simple set of words, then it had to acquire its own verse; and 'The Man I Love' resulted."[12]

Ira and George Gershwin by Al Hirshfeld San Diego Union, January 15, 1961.

Although that song was dropped from the show, "Fascinating Rhythm" survived and emerged as its greatest hit. George had written the first eight bars of the song while in England but finished it in New York. "It was a tricky rhythm for those days," recalled Ira, "and it took me several days to decide on the rhyme scheme. I didn't think I had the brilliant title in Fascinating Rhythm but A, it did sing smoothly, and B,—I couldn't think of a better." Ira and George argued for several days over whether some lines should have single or double rhymes. George won and double rhymes were adopted.[13] As noted by Michael Feinstein, the song "represented a style of music that hadn't been heard coming out of Tin Pan Alley before. Two elements make the song stand out: the accent changes on the notes for rhythmic effect and the shift of the accompaniment. It has a restless energy about it that quickens the pulse." The jagged phrases of the music competes with the lyric that still manages to anchor the song while maintaining "the carefree abandon of its syncopation."[14]

For the remainder of the 1920s, the Gershwin brothers wrote the words and music for *Tell me More* (1925), *Tip-Toes* (1925), and *Oh Kay!* (1926), from which came "Someone to Watch Over Me." "As originally conceived by the composer," remembered Ira, "this tune would probably not be around much today. . . .I would have written it up as another dance-and-ensemble number. One day, for no particular reason and hardly aware of what he was at, George started and continued it in a comparatively slow tempo; and half of it hadn't been sounded when both of us had the same reaction: this was really no rhythm tune but rather a wistful and warm one."[15]

"'S Wonderful" was a product of *Funny Face,* produced in 1927. As Ira later explained, his "principal reason for writing this lyric was to feature the sibilant sound effect by deleting the 'it' of 'it's' and slurring the leftover 's' with the first syllable of the following word. So I'm frequently baffled by what some singers have in mind and throat when they formalize the phrases to 'It's wonderful,' It's marvelous,' It's Paradise,' &."[16] Dorothy Parker, however, got it right. Evidently, she assumed those reading her short story "The Mantle of Whistler" would know that in their banter the characters were referring to the song:

> "What a Party this turned out to be!"
>
> "And how!" she said.
>
> "'And how' is right," he said. "'S wonderful."
>
> "'S marvelous," she said.
>
> "'S awful nice," he said.
>
> "'S Paradise," she said.[17]

Treasure Girl of 1928 resulted in no memorial songs. The following year, *Show Girl* opened, starring Ruby Keeler and Jimmy Durante. Produced by Florenz Ziegfeld, with the libretto by J. P. McEvoy, lyrics also by Gus Khan, and with the Duke Ellington orchestra providing the music, it seemed a sure hit, but it had a very short run. *Girl Crazy*, however, was another matter. From it came "Bidin' My Time," "But Not For Me," "Embraceable You," and "I Got Rhythm." The latter two had been previously written, and with a little editing were easily placed in the show. Regarding "I Got Rhythm," Ira admitted having difficulty coming up with a lyric that rhymed, so he found himself "not bothering with the rhyme scheme I'd considered necessary. . . .Though there is nothing remarkable about all this, it was a bit darning for me who usually depended on rhyme insurance." Because "who could ask for anything more" occurs four times, those lines would ordinarily determine the title of the song. But Ira found the first line of the chorus "sounded more arresting and provocative."[18] Ethel Merman, then twenty-one years old, launched "I Got Rhythm" in a way that guaranteed its success. Blessed with a powerful voice that carried to the back of an auditorium, she sent the audience into a frenzy by holding a high note for sixteen bars as the orchestra played the melody.[19]

The opening of *Girl Crazy* on October 14, 1930 saw a perfect convergence of jazz and the musical. The Red Nichols Orchestra, conducted that night by George Gershwin, included future jazz greats Jimmy Dorsey, Benny Goodman, Gene Krupa and Jack Teagarden, and even though they did not improvise, they most surely swung.[20] Moreover, "I Got Rhythm" became a jazz standard. These and many other artists of the Swing Era would play and record the song for most of their careers. And those who followed them into the modern jazz era often adopted the song's chord changes for their own compositions. Between 1930 and 1942, seventy-nine recordings were made of the song and songs based on its chords.[21]

Not as influential but certainly as recognizable, "Embraceable You" was introduced in *Girl Crazy* by Ginger Rogers. The song saw Ira returned to his forte, noting "some of its rhymes are four-syllable ones: 'embraceable you—replaceable you,' and (in a reprise) 'silk and laceable you'; 'tipsy in me—gypsy in me.' Also there is a trick four-syllable one in: 'glorify love—Encore!' if I love.'"[22] In "Bidin' My Time," Ira thought the song was too long and suggested to his brother that they cut out the second eight measures. Although "this version sounded a bit strange at first; but in a few days the eight-bar scissoring seemed to give the piece a more folksy validity."[23]

Ira had little to say about "But Not For Me," except that Rogers sang the song pessimistically and slowly after a lover's quarrel. Ira took it for granted that when those in the audience heard "With Love to Lead the Way/ I've found more Clouds of Gray/ Than any Russian Play/Could Guarantee" they would know that Russian plays are, indeed, "cloudy."[24] Ira would continue to offer cultural and historical allusions in his lyrics. Reviewing the show for the *New York Times*, a critic noted "George has written some good tunes, while Ira has provided tricky and ingratiating lyrics that should stimulate any ear surfeited with the usual rhyming insipidities of musical comedy."[25]

In November 1930, Ira commented on the difficulties the lyricist faced in an article in the *New York Times*. Thirty years ago the librettist usually wrote the lyrics for musical comedies, but lyric writing had become a profession: "A precarious profession, no doubt, . . .one that is looked down on as a racket in some literary fields, but one which, nevertheless, requires a certain dexterity with words and a feeling for music, on the one hand, and, on the other, the infinite patience of a gemsetter, compatibility with the composer and an understanding of the various personalities in the cast." He noted that only when P. G. Wodehouse began writing for Jerome Kern did critics realize that lyrics were worthy of attention. And once the lyricists realized that audiences actually paid attention to their lyrics, they strove to rise above the hackneyed and banal.[26]

Although he had written fifteen shows before *Girl Crazy*, Ira was quick to point out that the task got harder, not easier, because there was "so much one cannot repeat, so much snow of yesterday that is slush today, so many trick rhymes that have become second hand, so many titles that creak, and so few new angles on Jack and Jill, the Pied Piper and Little Goody Two-Shoes that working on a score and trying to set reasonable ideas to unreasonable rhythms becomes four months of intensive criss-cross word puzzling. However, what with a pot of black coffee at hand, a box of cigars in reach and a wolf at the door, one manages."[27]

The neglect of the lyricist was supposedly challenged by Mrs. Oscar Hammerstein when she heard someone claim "Ol' Man River" was a great Jerome Kern song. Not true, she said. Her husband wrote "Ol' Man River." Mr Kern wrote dum, dum dum, da.[28] Whether true or not, the story identifies the secondary role the lyricist was often accorded in the composition of a song. Because George Gershwin has received much more attention from critics and the public than has his brother, Mel Tormé complained "Ira got the short end of the stick. He seemed stuck in the shadow of his younger brother George." Yet it was Ira who created "some of the most engaging lyrics to be heard and sung."[29] Although the composer "must work with combination of only twelve notes," wrote Michael Feinstein, "but it's the job of the lyricist to ensure that the meaning of the song is distinctive. How do you come up with an original idea to differentiate your song from millions of love songs that have already been written? And if you have a catalogue of songs to your name, how do you make your next song different from the ones you've already written? And then how to write the one after that?"[30]

Ira was a stickler for the true or perfect rhyme, in which the penultimate or final accents of two words sound alike. Other forms of rhyming include near rhymes when either the vowel sounds are alike but the subsequent consonants are different or when the consonants sound alike but the accented vowels are different. As lyricist and composer Stephen Sondheim has noted, "A perfect rhyme snaps the word, and with it the thought, vigorously into place, rendering it easily intelligible; a near rhyme blurs it."[31] According to Ira, poets find the true rhyme too limiting and favor visual, suspended, and historical rhymes: "These are not, I feel, for the lyricist, whose output in the field of entertainment must be easily assimilable and whose work depends a good deal on perfect rhyme's jingle."[32]

Isaac Goldberg has analyzed the difficulties faced by the lyricist: "The composer has hit upon a tune that suggests a certain setting. It may be a 'hot' number, or a 'sweet' number, or a sentimental waltz. It has, then, a typical rhythm, which the lyric writer. . .must set to words. The wordsmith, working away from the composer, uses the unharmonized notes of the lead sheet as the pattern into which he must fit his lines and accents." This approach differed from an earlier period, "when it would have been possible, merely by looking at the printed words of a song, to form a fair idea of the musical setting—its rhythms, its structure, its design. The stanzas were regular; the lines were of even length. The song, in a word, was more or less predictable. Not today [1931]. The setting of words to a jazz-type melody forces the versifier to follow, in all its twists and turns, a jagged, capricious melodic line, and his ingenuity is kept on the alert, challenged to feats of dexterity. Seen by themselves, many of the stanzas look more foolish than they are; they do not readily suggest the music to which they have been often skillfully patterned."[33]

Following a "capricious melodic line" of a George Gershwin tune was not easy. After hearing the melody a few times, Ira could play it with one finger on the piano. He would give the song a title and then write the last line of the song which usually included the title. Ira got many of his titles from the argot of everyday conversation. Song titles such as "I Got a Crush on You," "Feeling I'm Falling," "Ka-ra-zy for You," and "High Hat" came from a the vernacular of the street. Hearing a comedian use words like "pash" for "passion" and "delish" for "delicious" inspired Ira to write half a dozen songs like "Sunny Disposish."[34]

Ira liked to end a song with a twist. For example, "Let's call the calling off off," ends "Let's Call the Whole Thing Off." As noted by Deena Rosenberg, "The best Gershwin songs are tiny one-act plays that encompass a satisfying, albeit brief, emotional and dramatic action, taking a character on a journey from one point, often stated in the title, to another, usually encapsulated in the last line."[35] Ira explained:

> The important thing about a lyric to me is the title and idea. You get an idea, you put it as a theorem in your title, you prove it, Q.E.D., to the listener's satisfaction in the lines that follow. . . .When people read poetry they can study the printed page, but each song lyric is hurled at them only once or twice in the course of an evening, and the audience has no chance to rehear or reread it. Thus, good lyrics should be simple, colloquial, rhymed, conversational lines. It is up to the lyric writer to take the few hundred words allotted him and use what ever ingenuity he has in turning them neatly and trying to get a phrase here and there which will get over to the customers in the theater and be quotable on the dance floor. But the song itself is the important thing, not the words or the music as separate entities.[36]

On another occasion Ira wrote: "Given a fondness for music, a feeling for rhyme, a sense of whimsy and humor, an eye for the balanced sentence, an ear for the current phrase, and the ability to imagine one self a performer trying to put over the number in progress—given all this, I still would say it takes four or five years collaboration with knowledgeable composers to become a well-rounded lyricist."[37] Oscar Levant commented on Ira's collaboration with his brother:

Theirs were talents that suffused and penetrated each other, paralleled and completed each other remarkably. Prior to his professional association with Ira, Gershwin's songs were rarely supplied with more than run-of-the-mill texts. The exceptions would be in favor of those he wrote with Irving Caesar and Buddy DeSylva. Ira's curious whimsicality and dryness, the brilliant finish and cohesion of his lyrics were a definite stimulus to George. One could not tire of the clean detail and effortless smoothness (in the final effect) of his texts.

Together they were interested, as a point of departure, in treating a thought, in evolving an idea. In their best work there is no compromise with traditional song-writing effects, no evidence of contentment either with echoing a manner devised by someone else or duplicating a coup they had evolved themselves. In consequence, the brightness of Ira's thought acted as a spur to George's musical resources and produced many songs that departed from the conventions they had found. They also strongly influenced others.

Rhythmically and formally the flow of Ira's verse frequently conditioned the turn of George's melodic and harmonic ideas.[38]

Ira never over-emphasized his contributions to the collaboration, but he hinted that his lyrics did not always come after the melody was written: "no rule obtains: sometimes its the lyrics, and sometimes the tune. And sometimes—more often than not these days—the words and music are written practically at the same time."[39]

On January 19, 1930, The *New York Times* announced that "GEORGE GERSHWIN has a brother. If you had not known this all along, you would have found it out Wednesday by the relative simple process of reading the reviews of 'Strike Up the Band.' . . . For in addition to the praise accorded the composer's versatile score, kind critical words were set upon paper on behalf of Brother Ira's deft, ingenious lyrics."[40] And because the show was a financial success, the Gershwins again joined with George S. Kaufman and Morrie Ryskind in a show that skewered the political establishment—*Of Thee I Sing*. The score of the show, noted John Kendrick, "displayed George Gershwin's patented blend of jazz and Broadway, with Ira building humorous musical scenes and finales in something like the style of Gilbert and Sullivan."[41]

Sondheim considered the show a good one because Ira was "in his element when he's writing satirical shows. . .where the push for far-out rhymes and wordplay is part of the fun."[42] An example of the wordplay is "Of Thee I Sing (baby)." As Ira recalled, "When we first played this sentimental political campaign song for those connected with the show, there were one or two strong objectors who thought that juxtaposing the dignified 'of thee I sing' with a slangy 'baby' was going a bit too far. Our response (a frequent one over the years) was that, naturally, we'd replace it with something else if the paying audience didn't take to it. This was one time we were pretty sure that they would; and they did. Opening night, and even weeks later, one could hear a continuous 'Of thee I Sing, Baby!' when friends and acquaintances greeted one another in the lobby at intermission time."[43]

Even though it did not become as popular with vocalists as with instrumentalists, it was the best song in a show that won the Pulitzer Prize in 1931. The first musical to be so honored, the prize went to Kaufman, Ryskind, and Ira, but not to George. The composer was excluded because it was a literary award.[44] Also excluded from any recognition was F. Scott Fitzgerald who claimed that Kaufman stole the idea of the show from his play, *The Vegetable*.[45]

Because *Of Thee I Sing* (as had *Strike up the Band*) integrated much of the music with the plot, the Gershwins wanted to continue writing this kind of show. And with *Porgy and Bess*, based on the book by DuBose Hayward, who also wrote some of the lyrics, they clearly achieved that goal. But the wonderful songs are so tied to the plot and sung in an Africa-American dialect that none but "Summertime" became a standard. *Porgy and Bess* failed to sway most critics at the time, but one wrote: "Owing to Mr. [Ira] Gershwin's valuable Broadway experience and partly to the superior singableness of the text, there is in *Porgy and Bess* little of that fatal discrepancy between word and note that has been the bane of American opera."[46] Stephen Sondheim favored the lyrics of Hayward over those of Ira because he used rhyme sparingly. Yet, he considered Ira's lyric to "Oh, Bess, Oh Where's My Bess?" simple, impressive and moving.[47]

While George was working on *Porgy and Bess*, Ira found the time to write songs with Yip Harburg and Harold Arlen for *Life Begins at 8:40*. The songs were not integrated into a plot, each being presented in a special dramatic and satirical setting. Sondheim favored "Let's Take a Walk Around the Block" because "it rides along with the effortless rhyming felicity he [Ira] so relentlessly pursued.[48] Unlike *Porgy and Bess*, *Life Begins at 8:40* had a successful run that only enhanced Ira's reputation, as if it needed enhancing.

In 1935, Ira Gershwin received an invitation to write the lyrics for a revival of the *Ziegfeld Follies*. Florenz Ziegfeld had died suddenly in 1932 deeply in debt, and Billie Burke, his widow, turned to the Shubert Brothers (J. J., Lee, and Sam) to produce the *Zeigfeld Follies* of 1936. They concluded that the new revue should be based less on a series of acts and numbers but on satire. The sketches were to be constructed around songs. When asked who he would like as the composer, Ira highly recommended Vernon Duke, with whom he had collaborated on *The Garrick Gaieties* of 1930.[49]

Once the contracts were signed, Ira, his wife Leonore, his brother George, Moss Hart, and Vernon Duke rented a house in Ocean Beach, on Fire Island, New York.[50] Lying off the southern shore of Long Island, it lacked electric lights and automobiles, and only two boats reached the island daily. It had become a colony of writers, composers, and stage personalities, which included dramatist Lillian Hellman, producer Billy Rose, and his wife Fanny Brice.[51]

Although the details of writing the songs and lyrics of a Broadway show are hardly the stuff that goes into an autobiography, fortunately Duke left us a brief but enticing account of how he and Ira, men of radically different temperaments and work habits, collaborated on the island:

> Ira's writing methods were slow and soothing and very restful. . . .Our work sessions usually began with a family dinner with Ira and Leonore, joined by Fanny Brice or Ellen [sic] Berlin. After a long copious meal, the company would repair to the drawing room, which housed the piano, and hectic conversation would ensue; I, on tenterhooks, would be dying to get to the piano and persuade Leonore and her guests to go elsewhere for their energetic gossip. I would shoot expressive glances at ever-placid Ira, who affected not to catch their meaning and willingly joined in the conversation. After an hour or so of this, I, totally exasperated, would invade the piano determinedly and strike a few challenging chords. This time Ira would heed my desperate call, stretch himself, emit a series of protracted sighs, say something to the effect that 'one had to work so-o-o hard for a living' and more in that vein, then interrupt himself to intone the magic word: 'However. . .' This 'however' meant that the eleventh hour had struck and the period of delicious procrastination was over. Ira, sighing pathetically, would then produce a small bridge table, various writing and erasing gadgets, a typewriter and four or five books, which he seldom consulted— Roget's Thesaurus, Webster's dictionary, rhyming dictionary, and the like—wipe and adjust his glasses, all these preparations at a molto adagio pace, and finally say in a resigned voice: 'O.K. Dukie. . .play that chorus you had last night.' After wrestling with last night's chorus for a half hour, Ira would embark on an ice-box raiding expedition, with me, fearful

of too long an interruption, in pursuit. There we'd stand in the kitchen, munching cheese and pickles, Ira obviously delighted with this escapist stratagem, I dutifully pretending to enjoy it too. Another sigh, another 'however,' then back to the piano. At 2 or 3 A.M. Ira would put away his working utensils and victoriously announce to Lee that he had completed four lines for the new chorus.[52]

Ira and Vernon.
Courtesy of The Ira and Lenore S. Gershwin Trusts.

Sometime during his collaboration with Ira, Vernon mentioned that he had written the melody and lyric to a song called "Face the Music with Me." Because it had never been produced or published, if Ira liked the melody he was encouraged to give it a new lyric. Ira liked it, gave it a new lyric, and called it "I Can't Get Started with You."[53]

Thus by chance, a song was rescued from oblivion. But neither the composer nor the lyricist had any idea if it would be included in the revue, live past the run of the show, or survive the economic upheaval called the Great Depression.

Chapter Four
The Song:
Typical But Unique

The Great Depression (1929-1939) nearly destroyed the music and entertaining communities. In 1932, six million records were sold, down from one-hundred million in 1927. The musicians' union lost one-third of its membership between 1928 and 1934.[1] In 1930 twenty-eight musicals opened; in 1933 only thirteen were staged.[2] The revues *Hellzapoppin* and *Pins and Needles* had very long runs, but only four musicals had more than 400 performances, one of them being *Anything Goes*. Music and lyrics by Cole Porter and starring Ethel Merman, it introduced "You're the Top," "I Get a Kick Out of You," and "Anything Goes."[3]

Although fewer shows were staged than in the 1920s, the best that survived were exceptional. The revues were less elaborate but often funnier; the musical comedies were better structured, although the runs of the shows were shorter. More black musicals and revues were staged during the early 1930s than during early 1920s. Six appeared in 1930-31, five the following season. They featured great local talent that would not have found employment elsewhere. Tryouts out-of-town were not necessary and touring was not an option. Sets, costumes, and labor costs were kept to a minimum, which appealed to producers, and most African American actors, musicians, and singers worked for lower salaries than did their white counterparts.[4]

But like the white musicals, the black shows had short runs. *Rhapsody in Black* had 80 performances, *Brown Buddies* 111.[5] With Bill Robinson tap dancing and Ada Brown singing "When a Black Man's Blue" and "Give Me a Man Like That," *Brown Buddies* was infused with elements of jazz and blues.[6] *Rhapsody in Black*, with songs from composers and lyricists such as George Gershwin, Dorothy Fields, and Jimmy McHugh and starring Ethel Waters, pleased everyone, including critics, in part because of its jazz components. Critic William F. McDermott noted that the "Pike Davis' Continental orchestra is a first-rate band for the playing 'blue' numbers." The orchestra also played Gershwin's "Rhapsody in Blue."[7]

Despite the star power of Robinson and Waters (and it was considerable), by the middle of the decade the black, like the white, musical was in decline. And the decline in the number of Broadway shows was in direct proportion to an increase in the number of movies produced after the advent of sound. Fewer shows meant fewer people were employed. And as the demand for movie musicals increased, increasing numbers of directors, choreographers, musicians, composers, and lyricists departed for Hollywood. Because the film industry also needed people who could enunciate and sing, who better than stage-trained actors?

Many of the "Ziegfeld Girls" (some being the daughters of police officers and saloon keepers) also headed west. Their chances of meeting and perhaps marrying wealthy men—the Stage Door Johnnies—declined as the Depression deepened. This led to the employment of women from a different strata—those who had graduated from high schools and colleges. They found friends, lovers, and husbands among the remaining actors and less affluent individuals in New York.[8]

Moving west as well, literally, were the songs of Tin Pan Alley. Understanding the importance of songs to the success of musicals, movie companies sought the copyrights of those they used. Warner Brothers bought out Witmark's, one of the Alley's biggest publishers, as did MGM with the Robbins Company. Other movie companies did the same. Because Irving Berlin owned his own music publishing company, he retained control over his songs but was the proverbial exception that proved the rule.[9]

Although Hollywood mainly wanted trite, conventional, escapist songs to cheer people up, now and then it acknowledged that the Depression actually existed. In the movie *Gold Diggers of 1933*, Ginger Rogers sings "We're in the Money," with an upbeat lyric that included "Old man depression, you are through/You done us wrong!/We never see a headline/'bout a breadline, today." More significantly, at the end of the movie Joan Blondell sings "Remember My Forgotten Man" by composer Harry Warren and lyricist Al Dubin. The sketch begins with Joan Blondell, a prostitute, offering her services to a man. He walks off and she introduces the song, lamenting what World War I had done to her man and thus to her. The use of "You" instead of "They" is accusatory:

Remember my forgotten man/You put

a rifle in his hand/

You sent him far away/ You shouted 'Hip horray'/

But look at him now."

Remember the forgotten man/You had him

cultivate the land/You had him work behind

a plow/The sweat fell from him brow/But

look at him now.

Etta Moten, an African American, repeats the song, and in a series of shots soldiers are happily marching off to war, then straggling back from the trenches, and finally standing in bread lines. Staged by Busby Berkeley in a style of German expressionism, it is one of Hollywood's finest moments. At the time, however, it may have been too much a reminder of the Depression. One reviewer wrote: "'My Forgotten Man,' unhappily placed at the end of the film, would have been better if he had remained forgotten though the score itself is melodious. Subsequent runs will do well to trim out three fourths of this sequence, which jars harshly upon the amusing note previously struck."[10]

Although Broadway did its best to ignore the Depression, there were a few exceptions, *The Cradle Will Rock*, music by Marc Blitzstein and directed by Orson Welles, being the most obvious example. A delightfully radical, pro-labor, but humorous tract, it was the subject of a movie of the same name made decades later about the staging of the play. Most Broadway shows, however, were much less serious and often introduced feel-good songs such as "On the Sunny Side of the Street" from Lew Leslie's *International Revue* of 1930. "I Found a Million Dollar Baby—In the Five and Ten-cent Store" was presented in Billy Rose's *Crazy Quilt* of 1931. And *George White's Scandals* of 1931-32 introduced "Life is Just a Bowl of Cherries." A song about hope, it ends with "The strongest oak must fall/The sweet things in life/To you were just loaned/So how can you lose what you've never owned?/Life is just a bowl of cherries/So live and laugh at it all."[11]

Slipped into the 1932 revue *Americana* was a serious song, similar in tone and intent to "Remember My Forgotten Man," that became the anthem of the Great Depression. "Brother Can You Spare a Dime" was written by Jay Gorney, with the lyric by E.Y. (Yip) Harburg. As recalled by Gorney, "I had a melody which Yip liked, but we couldn't get a title. . . .The melody had a plaintive note in it, and we wondered what a man would be sad about losing which he would sing about." While walking in Central Park, they were approached by a man who asked "Buddy, can you spare a dime." "'That's it,' said Yip. And we went right home and he wrote the lyric in about two hours."[12] Ironically, had the Depression not destroyed the electrical-supply company he worked for, Harburg probably would not have written the song, or any other for that matter: "The capitalists saved me in 1929, just as we were worth, oh, about a quarter of a million dollars. Bang! The whole thing blew up. I was left with a pencil, and finally had to write for a living."[13]

"Brother, Can You Spare a Dime," as explained by Harburg, expresses a man's "indignation over having worked hard in the system only to be discarded when the system had no use for him. . . . He's not sighing about it—he's feeling his strength, and brings that strength into the song. But suddenly he looks at himself and stops short, puzzled: 'How the hell did I get into this position.'"[14]

Once I built a railroad, I made it run

Made it race against time

Once I built a railroad, now it's done

Brother, can you spare a dime?

Once I built a tower up to the sun

Brick and rivet and lime

Once I built a tower, now it's done

Brother, can you spare a dime?

Once in khaki suits, gee we looked swell

Full of that Yankee Doodly-dum

Half a million boots went sloggin' through Hell

And I was the kid with the drum

Say, don't you remember, they called me "Al"

It was "Al" all the time.

Say, don't you remember, I'm your pal

Say, buddy can you spare a dime?[15]

According to Philip Furia, part of the lyric implies "that the same soldiers might now band together in revolutionary protest, an implication that hangs fire between the powerful, active verbs that recount the past—'built a tower, 'made it run,' 'went slogging through hell'—and the participles 'standing' and 'waiting' that uneasily mark time for the present. The suggestion of revolution grows stronger with the reference to 'Yankee-Doodle-de-dum' and the allusion to the 'Spirit of 76'—'I was the kid with the drum.'"[16]

Bing Crosby recorded the song with Brunswick three weeks after *Americana* opened, and within two weeks it was the best selling record in the U.S. Columbia Records produced a Rudy Vallee version, and Al Jolson also recorded it. But it was Crosby's version that captured the nation. As strongly expressed by his biographer, it was "a perfectly pitched statement of protest and empathy, dignified but not somber, rueful but not bitter, heroic but not overwrought."[17] Given its historical context and dark theme, "Brother Can You Spare a Dime" was hardly the kind of song that would be repeatedly sung over the years. But it was written during the golden-age of the American popular song, many of them coming from Broadway shows.

The Broadway song of the period usually follows a well worn path. It often begins with a verse, a phrase of sixteen bars that introduces the theme, the mood, the tempo, and rhythm of a song.[18] It also prepares the listeners for the body of the song—the chorus, also called the refrain. To many record producers, however, the verse extended the song too long for the restraints of a 78rpm record and a radio broadcast. The decline in the sales of sheet music during the Depression may also have led songwriters to forgo the verse.[19]

As noted by Mel Tormé, "In the Thirties and Forties, the verse to a song sometimes set the chorus up so that, without that frontispiece, the tune was actually incomplete."[20] For example, the verse to "Star Dust" ends with an unresolved situation: "Love is now the star dust of yesterday/The music of the years gone by." By the end of the chorus, however, things have changed: "Ah but that was long ago/Now my consolation/Is in the star dust of a song." When sung without the verse "I Guess I'll Have to Change My Plan" is simply about a young man who concludes that the woman he loves is in love with another man, so he must change his plan. With the verse, however, the song takes on a deeper meaning, because from it we learn that the woman is married and perhaps has led him on.

Vernon Duke thought dispensing with the verse a great pity, because some "Kern, Gershwin and Rodgers verses have greater musical inventiveness and charm than the strait-jacketed refrain."[21] According to Alec Wilder, "it's in the verses that the writer should be freer, for in practical terms it's the chorus that's being sold or promoted. So if the writer wishes to break loose, that is, if he is talented enough to, that's the place to do it."[22] Probably to snag the listener's attention, in some recordings the chorus is sung first, followed by the verse. This, of course, upends the song's intent and structure.

The chorus resolves, or should resolve, the situation stated in the verse. In most American popular songs, the chorus consists of thirty-two bars divided into four eight-bar sections. Many, if not most, follow an AABA formula. The main theme of the song is stated in the first A section and is repeated in the second. The B part, called the bridge, or release, relieves the repetition by modulating to another key. It usually takes the melody in a new direction. If the melody has descended, the bridge might ascend. The lyric might change from joy to sadness. The final A returns to the main theme and takes the song to its conclusion, sometimes with a tag ending.

Philip Furia acknowledged the AABA formula (and versions of it) puts the lyricist in a straitjacket and admitted that to many listeners the lyrics of modern popular songs tend to sound the same. But "we must listen, not for new ideas or deep emotions, but for the deftness which the lyricist solves the problem posed by a song of the 1930s." Lorenz Hart, Cole Porter, and Ira Gershwin solved the problem by introducing a world-weary skepticism to their work, with phrases such as "this can't be love," "it was just one of those things," and "how long has this been going on?" Their lyrics are urbane, sophisticated, stylish, and witty.[23]

Not all critics found the songs worthy of the praise they often received. Writing for the *Boston Herald* in 1939, Alexander Williams claimed that in form and harmony the popular song contains "severe limitations which can be broken only at the risk of the popularity that must at all costs be cultivated." Because the songs were designed to be sung or whistled by "the man on the street," the range is usually limited to just over an octave, to the tenth of the scale. Jerome Kern's "Smoke Gets in Your Eyes" may be an exception in that its range is nearly two octaves, but it is difficult to sing. Moreover, harmonically most popular songs rely on certain chromatic chords with sentimental qualities: the raised fifth, the added sixth, the augmented sixth, successions of primary and secondary sevenths, the primary ninth, all of which are "used in very obvious fashion." He praised Vernon Duke for the uniqueness of his verse to "Where Have We met Before," which is divided into two sections of seven bars each, but then criticized him for reverting to the same old AABA form. Williams concluded by insisting "the popular song composer is severely limited in what he may and may not do." Although some of the songs possess charm and vitality, they nevertheless lack originality.[24]

"I Can't Get Started" possesses charm, vitality, *and* originality. Copyrighted in 1935 by Chappell & Co., the sheet music consists of a rather simple piano arrangement with chord symbols for ukulele, guitar, and banjo. More than the arrangement, the symbols clearly identify the age of the sheet music, they being of the simplest kind that mostly used the open strings of the instruments. It is, moreover, the perfect example of the AABA formula. The chorus begins with a Cma7 arpeggio in the I VI, II7, V7 chord progression which is typical of many popular songs.

It is the bridge, however, that makes the song unique. Alec Wilder found it "extremely ingenious" in its repeated return to the whole note A but each time supported by different harmony. He also pointed out that through the years, singers and players have altered the bridge by changing the F sharp to a F natural in the third measure and by changing the last E natural to an E flat in the last measure.[25] In succeeding publications of the sheet music, numerous substitute chords have been introduced. Regarding the bridge, in the original sheet music the first "A" is supported by an Em7 chord, the second by a D, and the third by a Dm7. Substituted chords would look like this: the first "A" is backed up by an Em11(the eleventh being the melody note), the second "A" by a DMa9 (the fifth being the melody note) and the third "A" by a G9sus (the ninth being the melody note).[26]

The originality of the bridge, however, may account for the uniqueness of the verse being overlooked by those analyzing the song. The first eight measures are in the key of C. But it modulates to the key of E for the next five measures before returning to C. Like the bridge, the verse reflects the mind of a highly trained classical musician.

The lyric has undergone significant changes over the years, but the first one is arguably the best. Except for playfully changing the pronunciation of "profile" to "pro-feel" so it would rhyme with "feel," Ira strictly adhered to his policy of using only true rhymes.

The Verse

I'm a glum one; it's explainable:

I met someone unattainable;

Life's a bore,

The world is my oyster no more.

All the papers, where I led the news

With my capers, now will spread the news:

"Superman Turns Out to Be Flash in the Pan."

First Chorus

I've flown around the world in a plane;

I've won the race from Newport to Maine;

The North Pole I have charted,

But can't get started with you.

Around a golf course I'm under par,

The Theatre Guilders want me to star;

I've got a house—a show-place—

But I get no place with you.

(Bridge)

Your so supreme,

Lyrics I write of you; Scheme

Just for the sight of you; Dream

Both day and night of you,

And what good does it do?

I've been consulted by Franklin D.

And Greta Garbo's asked me to tea,

And I'm brokenhearted
'Cause I can't get started with you.

Second Chorus
I do a hundred yards in ten flat;
The Duke of Kent has copied my hat;
With queens I've à la carted,
But can't get started with you.

When Democrats are all in a mess,
I hear Jim Farley's call of distress,
And I help him maneuver,
But I'm just Hoover to you.

(Bridge)
When first we met—
How you elated me! Pet!
Now you've devastated me! Yet,
Now you've deflated me
Till you're my Waterloo.

When J. P. Morgan bows, I just nod;
Green Pastures wanted me to play God.
The Siamese Twins I've parted,
But I can't get started with you.

Third Chorus
The Himalaya Mountains I climb;
I'm written up in Fortune and Time.
New Yorker did my profile ["pro-feel"]
But I've had no feel from you.

There's always "Best regards and much love"

From Mr. Lehman—you know the Gov;

I go to ev'ry state ball,

But I'm behind the eight ball with you.

      (Bridge)

Oh tell me why

Am I no kick to you? I,

Who'd always stick to you? Fly

Though thin and thick to you?

Tell me why I'm taboo!

Oh, what a man you're keeping at bay;

I use a pound of Lifebuoy each day;

But you've got me downhearted

'Cause I can't, I can't, I can't, I can't

I can't get started with you.[27]

      Common in the Broadway songs of the times were allusions to contemporary or historical persons, events, and even products. The lyricists relied on the knowledge and sophistication of their audience to understand the wit and satire. Regarding Ira's lyric to "They All Laughed," Michael Feinstein, singer and lover of standards, noted how "dated" the allusions to the Wright Brothers, Guglielmo Marconi, Eli Whitney, Robert Fulton, and Henry Ford had become: "The historical references in the song get more obscure with each passing year. Unfortunately, the name dropping that lends this lyric its originality and inventiveness now makes the song increasingly inaccessible to generations of kids who are no longer taught who Whitney or Fulton were."[28]

The allusions made in "I Can't Get Started" clearly date the song and some of them probably tax the memories of those who lived during the 1930s. Even historian Ted Gioia, who loves the song, noted that the lyric now seems "quaintly passé," although it works "well enough in performance."[29] But I find quaint and passé to be positive characteristics. Whether fully understood or not, the lyric, like a historical document, informs us today what people in 1935 found relevant, interesting, and amusing. According to jazz critic Leonard Feather, since the beginning of the twentieth century, the lingua franca of America has been the popular song: "Through its lyrics we can detect beliefs and fads and fashions; its melodies reflect our aesthetic values, for better or worse."[30]

Consequently, an explanation of the lyric to "I Can't Get Started" is in order. Although the allusions refer to people and events in the Great Depression, the great event is not mentioned, probably intentionally. Flying around the world in a plane was a remarkable feat in 1936, the first to do so being Wiley Post in 1933. The Newport to Maine race refers to a famous yacht regatta. The Theatre Guiders were members of a theatrical society that produced plays. Franklin D was the loving moniker attached to President Franklin Delano Roosevelt. Greta Garbo, the famous Swedish film actress, starred in *Anna Karenina* in 1935. The Duke of Kent refers to English royalty. J. P. Morgan was a famous financier. *Green Pastures* was a popular stage play with an all black cast that was filmed in 1936. Jim Farley was a New York politician and kingmaker. Hoover was President Herbert Hoover during the 1929 stock-market crash and Napoleon was the guy who lost the Battle of Waterloo. *Fortune, Time,* and *The New Yorker* were popular publications. Herbert H. Lehman was governor of New York from 1933 to 1942. The phrase "Am no kick to you" acknowledges Cole Porter's "I Get a Kick out of You." Lifebuoy was a well known soap of the times.

In the published version of the song, part of the lyric was changed because the times had changed. "I won the race from Newport to Maine" became "I've settled revolutions in Spain." Although this seems to refer to the Spanish Civil War, the war did not begin until 1936. One explanation is that the words then referred to a strike of miners in the northern Spanish region of Asturias in October 1934. The strike was brutally put down by General Francisco Franco, who went on to lead the rebellion against the democratic government. Once the war began, the words nicely fit the new reality.

To prevent legal action, references to institutions, persons and products were also eliminated. The first allusions better locate the song in the 1930s than do their replacements, and without them much of the satire and charm of the piece is lost. Thus, "The Theatre Guilders want me to star" became "And all the movies want me to star." "I've been consulted by Franklin D. And Greta Garbo's asked me to tea" metamorphosed into "In 1929 I sold short; In England I'm presented at court." In the second chorus, "The Duke of Kent has copied my hat" correctly became "The Prince of Wales has copied my hat," a reference to Prince Edward Albert who brought the bowler back into style in England and who greatly influenced fashion in the United Kingdom. Because Edward Albert became King Edward VIII in early 1936, however, Ira's new stanza became quickly dated. The stanza that begins with "While Democrats are all in a mess" was changed to "The leading tailors follow my styles. And toothpaste ads all feature my smiles/The Astrobilts I visit/But say, what is it with you." Rhyming "visit" with "what is it" clearly demonstrates Ira's masterly use of colloquial American-English. He got around the "censors" by combining the famous Astor and Vanderbilt families into the Astrobilts. The stanza that begins with "When J. P. Morgan bows" was discarded for "I've sold my kisses at a bazaar/And after me they named a cigar/But lately, how I've smarted—"Cause I can't get started with you." The ending of the third chorus was changed from "Cause I can't, I can't, I can't, I can't, I can't get started with you" to simply "'Cause I can't get started with you."

The lyric of the bridge, however, remained unchanged and is the most creative part of the song. According to Furia, "with the persistent return to the same whole note, the music itself can't get started, and Gershwin matches it with equally sputtering rhymes that interrupt, rather than advance the syntax:

You're so supreme—

lyrics I write of you, scheme—

just for the sight of you, dream—

both day and night of you

All these false starts then explode in the exasperated 'And what good does it do?'—another instance of Ira Gershwin's knack of placing an utterly simple catch-phrase at an emotional climax, giving vernacular luster to both phrase and setting."[31]

"I Can't Get Started" is a typical "catalogue song," in which the lyric lists how much someone loves someone else. A perfect example, is "All the Things You Are" by Jerome Kern: "You are the promised kiss of springtime/that makes the lonely winter seem long/You are the breathless hush of evening/that trembles on the brink of a lovely song." And so on. I like the melody better than the lyric, which seems a bit over the top, but in the context of its presentation in the 1939 Broadway show *Very Warm for May*, it may have been beautifully presented. The words and music of Cole Porter, however, need no context in which to be appreciated. Clearly, he was the master of the catalogue song that is amply demonstrated in "You're the Top." In the words of Philip Furia, the song "bubbles over in a rapid-fire list of images and allusions that threatens to go on endlessly."[32] Porter's juxtaposition of tourist attractions, famous artists and even a mouse is unique: "You're the top/You're the Colosseum/ You're the top/You're the Louvre Museum/You're a melody from a symphony by Strauss/ You're a bandel hornet/A Shakespeare sonnet/You're Mickey Mouse."

Catalogue songs, especially those of Porter, lent themselves to parody: "You're the top/You're Miss Pinkham's tonic/You're the top/You're a high colonic/You're a burning heat of a bridal suite in use/You're the breasts of Venus/You're King Kong's penis/ You're self-abuse." Usually credited to Porter, the lyric may have come from Irving Berlin.[33] If so, it is refreshing to know that the composer of "God Bless America" had a wicked side to him. More than imitation, parody may be the sincerest form of flattery. "You're the Top" is a perfect example of a song of great wit with no serious content having a long life after its initial performance.

"I Can't Get Started" was also written with great wit and was intended to be nothing more than comical show tune. Indeed, the way it was first presented suggests it was not to be taken very seriously at all.

Chapter Five
The Ziegfeld Follies:
More for the Eye than the Ear

Those hired by Harry Kaufman, the manager-in-chief of the production of the *Ziegfeld Follies* of 1936, were a virtual "who's who" (or soon would be) of the musical theater. Vernon Duke composed the score. Ira Gershwin wrote the lyrics and although not credited contributed ideas and material for the sketches. Director John Murray Anderson had introduced the revolving stage, and was well known as an innovator in the use of movement, color, and design. He had directed numerous revues, including the *Ziegfeld Follies* of 1934. Vincente Minnelli, who began his career as a designer for *Earl Carroll's Vanities* of 1931, was hired to design the sets and costumes. He would go on to direct many films, marry Judy Garland, and father a well known performer known as Liza. In his Broadway debut, Russian-born George Balanchine created the ballet sequences. An important choreographer in Europe before emigrating to the United States, he would later organize the New York City Ballet Company and direct it for many years. Robert Alton arranged the dance numbers, and H. I. Phillips, Moss Hart, and David Freedman wrote the sketches. Hart was a librettist and sketch-writer of several musicals. He also authored non-musical plays such as *You Can't Take it With You*, and *The Man who Came to Dinner*, both made into movies.[1] Freedman wrote sketches for musicals and still found the time to write a play, short stories, novels, and biographies of Eddie Cantor and with Cantor of Florenz Ziegfeld. Because the sketches were inflated anecdotes, he claimed they were as difficult to write as plays. In a few pages they had to convey what a play did in three acts. And if the last line did not work, the sketch failed.[2]

Regarding the performers, Fanny Brice was in the *Follies* of 1910, and beginning in 1916 she starred in seven *Ziegfeld Follies*.

Famously known as a Jewish-accented clown, a tear-jerking ballad singer, and the naughty child Baby Snooks, she had introduced several songs that became well known, including "My Man." Comedian Eve Arden performed in the 1934 edition of the *Follies* and in *Parade* the following year. She would go on to appear in other shows, a television series, and about sixty movies, often as the sarcastic, wise-cracking pal of the leading lady. Already known for his work in *Roberta* of 1933, Bob Hope would become world famous for his radio shows, movie roles, television performances, and for his overseas tours to entertain U.S. military forces.[3] Vernon Duke found Bob Hope "a most engaging young man, with a freshly scrubbed, balcony-nosed face, rather self-effacing compared with our trio of female prima donnas and always worried about his waistline."[4]

The original cast also included Hugh O'Connell, Cherry and June Preisser, the tap-dancing Nicholas Brothers (Fayard and Herold), ballerina Harriet Hoctor, and Gertrude Niesen. The latter was not a Broadway performer but a radio singer under contract with the Columbia network. She chose to join the cast of the *Follies* because radio work prevented her from developing her acting skills. Experience on the stage would correct that neglect. Working with the director John Murray Anderson may also have been a factor in her decision, as was the opportunity to sing the songs of Gershwin and Duke.[5] But not everyone was happy with her decision. According to Duke, Niesen "found fault with everybody and everything." He also mentioned that the producers had signed "a genuine Paris importation, Mlle. Josephine Baker, originally of Harlem. La Baker, with a French count in tow, two beautifully groomed dogs of exotic appearance and a large assortment of the best Vuitton luggage, received us majestically in her hotel suite."[6] Before relocating to Paris, Baker, as a member of the chorus, had appeared in the 1922 production of *Shuffle Along.*

Beside the stars, the cast consisted of seventy-five other performers, many being ballerinas who lived apart from the rest of the cast. Their captain, Evelyn Dale, told a newspaper reporter "We must have mental, as well as physical co-ordination. A family spirit of

Cast of The Follies - Boston Herald, December 29, 1935
Top: Bob Hope and Hugh O'Connel; Middle: Fanny Brice;
Bottom: Gertrude Niesen and Josephine Baker

affection, mental understanding, kindred tastes and purpose must be preserved." None of the ballerinas could stay out after midnight, which meant they never stayed out that late because the revue ended at 11:30. By emphasizing that her "girls have a fine standard of breeding and refinement," Dale may have been implying that other members of the cast were lacking in these characteristics.[7] The curfew obviously "protected" the dancers, perhaps to their dismay, from the advances of Stage Door Johnnies.

The show officially opened at the Boston Opera House on December 25, 1935. It begins with "Time Marches On." Performed by Bob Hope, it pokes fun at previous *Follies*:

Ladies and gentlemen,

Just because you don't see me

surrounded by a bevy of beautiful squaws,

Don't get the impression this isn't the

Ziegfeld Follies because

It's the *Follies* all right, but on a

basis entirely new:

We feel that the day of the girly-girly

    show is definitely through

In fact we even have a song about it.

Sing it boys.

"The California Varsity Eight," a chorus, then offers:

    Gone is the day of the show girl

    Where charms captivate the Don Juan;

    This year we cater to no girl—

    Time marches on!

Hope and the chorus exchange stanzas until the end when Hope is surrounded by beautiful girls and emotes "Aw the hell with it."[8]

Boston Herald, December 15, 1935

    Following the opening came a series of sketches, dances, and songs. Boston audiences were especially privileged to see a sketch that included a dance staged by Balanchine, costumes designed by Minnelli, and a song sung by Judy Canova. As "Maw," she sang "The Ballad of Baby Face McGinty (Who Bit Off More Than he

75

Could Chew)" to her three bearded sons in a Kentucky cabin about a gangster modeled on Baby Face Nelson, Machine Gun Kelly and Al Capone. Each stanza began with the lights coming up on a darkened cabin and recounts an event in McGinty's life. At age seven, he stole his grandmother's false teeth to get some gin. At twenty-one, he ruled St. Louis, holding up a bank every day and dealing in booze. He killed, raped, and murdered until arrested for not paying his income taxes. As the lights went up on the last stanza, the entire cast sang "So long, good-bye, McGinty/On one thing you were lax/You could get away with murder/But not on your income tax."[9]

The performance, recalled Duke, although "imaginatively staged by Balanchine, was inexplicably dropped in Boston."[10] Ira thought it was "a stunner," but understood it was cut, not because it needed work which was the usual explanation. It was cut because "there was a more than usual amount of comedy; there were plenty of stageable songs and special material (because of production postponements Duke and I had been at it eight or nine months, and twenty-five numbers were available). . . .But we had too much show with too many elaborate production numbers." Consequently, "unless you are Richard Wagner or Eugene O'Neill, overlength has to be considered. The Show Must Go On—but not too long after eleven p.m."[11]

Elinor Hughes, theater critic for the *Boston Herald*, was not very enthusiastic about the production and its performers. Josephine Baker was a "supple, panther-like young woman whose personality is of more importance than her singing and dancing." Harriet Hoctor performed "some attractive ballets, particularly 'Night Fright,' but she was rather submerged by the overwhelming size of the production." Gertrude Niesen sang two ballads, "Moment of Moments," and "Words without Music," songs Hughes thought would become the most popular numbers in the production. But the show "must be cut, pruned and provided with more comedy. All this undoubtedly sounds like unkind carping, but with such an abundance of talents combined, it was only natural to expect something exceptional. . . .It is the mundane material of sketches and songs that disappoint." She ended her review by noting "The celebrated Ira Gershwin, the even more famous Vernon Duke and Moss Hart did a lot of lyrics, music and sketches but it was an evening for the eye, not the ear."[12]

On February 1, 1936, the show opened on Broadway at the Winter Garden, but, according to Duke, it was marked by Josephine Baker's "unprecedented but, I fear, not unprefabricated triumph. The entire balcony was filled with her friends and admirers, and they made such a din at their idol's merest apparition, that no one, not even the audience-proof Fanny, could follow amidst the frenzied cheering accorded La Baker." Duke considered her a "woman of indefinable talents—she's no trained dancer, an inaudible singer and certainly no comedienne in the American sense."[13]

Despite the competition, Fanny Brice went on to steal the show, especially her singing of "He Hasn't a Thing Except Me." The sketch opens with a forlorn Brice leaning against a lamppost. The lamppost walks off and after the verse, Brice sings: "I give you his highness/A pain worse than sinus/Though I felt all hopped up/The minute he popped up/It's easy to see/He hasn't a thing except me." In the middle of the second chorus she stops singing and addresses the audience as herself, an audience that was clearly familiar with her history of singing about men:

> Well you get the idea. You know, I've been
> singing about this kind of bum for twenty-five
> years. Sometimes he's called 'Oh My Gawd, I
> Love Him So!' Or 'He's Just My Bill.' Or
> 'You Made Me What I am Today.' Once he
> was even called "the Curse of an Aching
> Heart.' But he's always the same lowlife and
> he's always doing me dirt and I just keep on
> loving him. Can you imagine if I really ever
> met a guy like that, what I would do to him?

Why, I'd. . . .It's no use talkin'. That' my type.

The conductor raps impatiently. Fannie gets back into character.[14]

Ira considered Fanny "one of the most versatile and accomplished personalities in our musical theater. In this particular *Follies*, for example, she put over this torch song, and did a wonderful burlesque of modern dancing, following her singing of Modernistic Moe. In the skits she played Baby Snooks; then a tough Tenth Avenue' girl then the most elegant English drawing-room matron in 'Fawncy, Fawncy;' then a Bronx housewife who has misplaced her winning Sweepstakes ticket; then a starlet in a satire of Hollywood musicals—all exquisitely and incomparably executed."[15]

According to a critic, however, little had been done to improve the revue. It consisted of a "mosaic of pageantry, dancing spectacle, girls and a modicum of comedy. And the girls are beautiful." The paucity of comedy was no fault of Fanny Brice, who was everywhere in sketches, burlesques, and "in song she is just about the stoutest prop the show has." The reviewer acknowledged "Ira Gershwin's lyrics are saucy and witty. Vernon

Bob Hope and Fanny Brice
Courtesy of The Ira and Lenore S. Gershwin Trusts.

Duke's score is pretty but not spectacular."[16] If the show offered nothing but Fanny Brice, wrote Brooks Atkinson of *The New York Times*, "most of us would feel sufficiently grateful." He thought the songs by Duke were "probably all right," and "Gertrude Niesen sings most of them with a cloudy voice suggesting an oboe with a cold, and probably that is all right, too."[17]

Duke noted in his autobiography that the "second Shubert *Follies* was a better show than the first, thanks to Minnelli, Balanchine and Anderson. . . , but somehow, perhaps owing to the performers, the score didn't come off too impressively in the theater." He was most impressed with Fanny Brice, especially in "The Gazooka," in which she appeared as "Ruby Blondell," a cross of Ruby Keeler and Joan Blondell. The "Gazooka," was a dance that parodied the "Carioca," the "Continental," and other film-created dance crazes, and was announced as done in "Techinquecolor" and on "Widescope Screen." Duke enthused that Gershwin and David Freedman were eighteen years ahead of their time and "proved a regular pair of Nostradamuses in this opus."[18]

The prominence of Brice put Josephine Baker at a disadvantage. Duke and Ira wrote her two highly spiced tropical arias—"5 A.M." and "Maharanee." And even though Duke was hardly a fan, he admitted she "mastered the acrobatic intervals and larynx-defying trills like a trouper, although she was seldom audible."[19] Regarding "Five A.M," the scene opens with Baker, playing a young women—clearly a prostitute—reclining on a sofa in a silver sequins gown. She reflects on her evening out:

Five A.M. And I am home again. Five A.M.

Five A.M. My time is my own again. Five A.M.

Through with the night I slave in,

I'm in my haven at last.

Through with a smile that is deceiving

The make-believing is past.

Home again. No white tie is facing me. Home again.

No Don Juan embracing me. Home again.

Soon enough the masquerade starts again—

Soon enough I'm playing with hearts again—

Five A.M.

I live in a world of my own.

As she sings, Baker is surrounded by dancers in an erotic dream sequence, choreographed by Balanchine, that combines modern dance and ballet. Baker glides through the dancers and then returns to the sofa to finish the song.[20]

Ira may have been announcing to Cole Porter he too could write about illicit love. "Topping" one another was a good-natured game many of the lyricists played. But Porter's "Love for Sale," was considered so indecent in 1930 that it was banned from the airwaves for several years. Why "Five A.M." produced no such reaction in 1936 is difficult to understand. But a little "bad" publicity might have brought the song the attention it richly deserved. Biographer Lawrence D. Stewart considered "5 A.M" Vernon's "most imaginative and extensive work for this *Follies*."[21]

Stewart also had high praise for "Words without Music," claiming that Ira had not only written the lyric but had created the melodic theme as well: "Duke took it down, developing it with his own special phrasing and harmonies."[22] To Philip Furia the song possesses all the qualities of a potential standard. Ira "discerned in brief musical phrases overtones of incompleteness and unfulfillment, which he then made articulate in haunting nostalgic images."[23]

Words without music,

Smoke without flame—

Charming phrases

That sing your praises

And call your name

Nights without magic,

Days without end—

Same old story,

The empty glory

Of let's Pretend.[24]

Because his brother's "music seldom resonated with such world-weary heartache, Ira's ability to adapt his lyric to Duke's cosmopolitan, melancholy style is another tribute to his collaborative powers," noted Furia.[25] Late in his life, Ira wrote: "You can count on the fingers of one hand, and perhaps the thumb and index finger on the other, the number of our theater composers whose melodic line and harmonies are highly individual. There is no question but that Vernon Duke must be considered one of these. Although 'Words without Music' is scarcely known—and therefore not in the class of 'April in Paris,' 'Autumn in New York,' 'I Can't Get Started,' 'What is There to Say?' and many others—it is an excellent example of Duke's distinctive style."[26] Evidently, the producers of the show thought highly of "Words without Music," because they put it in the first half of the production. As explained by Isaac Goldberg, a song the producers saw as a possible hit would be placed in the show where it would have the most affect: "Occurring too soon, it may like fireworks explode prematurely; occurring too late it may lose by anticlimax."[27]

That "I Can't Get Started" was placed in the second half of the revue, next to the last song sung, suggests that no one thought it had a chance of becoming a hit, even though it was introduced by Bob Hope. To many it might seem ironic that Hope, better known for his wise cracking than his singing, was the first to formally present the song in public. But Hope possessed a perfect-pitch tenor well-suited popular songs, as his singing of "Thanks for the Memory" in the film *The Big Broadcast of 1938* clearly demonstrates. Winner of the academy award for the best song of 1938, it became Hope's signature song. He would conclude his radio and later television shows with a stanza of it.

In the *Follies* sketch, Hope and Eve Arden, in evening clothes, are standing on a street corner. She hails passing cabs but none stops.

HOPE: Wasn't it a wonderful dinner?

ARDEN: Oh, all right. I've had better. Well Good night.

She starts to leave

HOPE: Wasn't it funny how the customers

recognized me? You know, I had to

sign twenty autographs.

ARDEN: So what? Well, good night. Here, taxi!

HOPE: Gosh, I can't seem to get to first base

with you. Never a smile, never a kind

word. Good God, what would I have to

give you for a kiss?

ARDEN: Ronald Colman.

HOPE: You know, we were in the same class at Oxford.

ARDEN: Well, you're not in his class now.

HOPE: Listen, on six continents and seven

oceans, I'm tops. Everyone's crazy

about me. And I'm crazy about you. I

love you so, I want you so.

ARDEN: So what? Well—

BOTH: Good night.[28]

The orchestra now introduces the song, and Hope sings the verse and the choruses. By the time he finished, Arden had warmed up to him. Hope plants a long kiss, and she calls him marvelous. That is all he wanted to know. Hope jauntily exists and the stage goes dark.[29]

Most critics failed to mentioned "I Can't Get Started," but Duke identified "Ibee" of *Variety* as the "real discoverer" of the song he called the show's hit.[30] For obvious reasons, John Anderson of *Time* mentioned the song and the stanza that included "The Himalaya Mountains I climb/I'm written in Fortune and Time."[31] Interestingly, historian of musicals Ethan Mordden claimed the song "defines celebrity as a form of entitlement: the man bigger than J. P. Morgan merits the girl of his choice, and she's supposed to know that."[32] But this makes sense only in the context of the sketch. Apparently, Mordden was unfamiliar with the song's long history and the variety of ways it has been interpreted.

Eve Arden and Bob Hope
Courtesy of The Ira and Lenore S. Gershwin Trusts.

Mordden's criticism of the song, however, pales to that levied at Josephine Baker. John Anderson wrote: "In sex appeal to jaded Europeans of the jazz-loving type, a Negro wench always has a head start. The particular tawny tint of tall and stringy Josephine Baker's bare skin stirred French pulses. But to Manhattan theatre-goers last week she was just a slightly buck-toothed young Negro woman whose figure might be matched in any night club now, whose dancing & singing could be topped practically anywhere outside France."[33] Other critics were less critical but barely so. According to Brooks Atkinson, "Josephine Baker has become a celebrity who offers her presence instead of her talent. They have given her a ravishing setting, effulgent gowns or practically no costume at all, which is an improvement, but her singing voice is only a squeak in the dark and her dancing is only the pain of an artist. Miss Baker has refined her art until there is nothing left in it."[34] As the 1935 French film *Princess Tam-Tam* clearly demonstrates, Josephine Baker danced with far more exuberance than ability, but it is difficult to believe the viewers cared.

In her autobiography, Baker admitted she did not go over well. She found it impossible to compete with Fanny Brice, "an immensely appealing figure," who was married to producer Billy Rose and who had twenty-five years of show business experience. Far from always being fully dressed in her Paris routines, she nevertheless considered herself to be "nothing but a body to be exhibited in various stages of undress."[35] Her "color may have stacked the odds against her success in America," noted her biographer, "but it is also true that Brice, with a nervous energy and funny-girl appeal so similar to Baker's, was already doing the act with which Baker could best have pleased an American audience."[36]

Brice was so important that when she came down with laryngitis the show was closed on February 3 and 4, only four days after it had opened. She rejoined the cast on the fifth. And on the twenty-ninth, she and select members of the cast performed sketches and sang songs in *The Ziegfeld Follies of the Air*, a weekly CBS broadcast that would continue for the next three months. The Al Goodman orchestra provided the music. Apparently, the show

Josephine Baker
Courtesy of The Ira and Lenore S. Gershwin Trusts.

served to introduce new songs, "You, Only You" being presented in an April broadcast. It was written not by Ira and Vernon but rather by Freddie Ahlert and Joe Young.[37]

In early May, because arthritis of the leg, Brice again withdrew from the show, forcing it to close for several months. In June, Harry Kaufman ordered Vernon to write some new songs for the show when it reopened. He and the lyricist Ted Fetter (Ira had left for California) would have first crack at incorporating them, provided they were as good or better than those provided by their

Boston Herald, February 29, 1936

competitors. But behind their backs, Kaufman bought five pieces from publishers and immediately put them into rehearsal, with only one Duke/Fetter song. It was withdrawn three days later. Although Vernon's contract clearly stated that no interpolations would be allowed unless approved by Ira and himself, friends persuaded him not to rock the boat.[38]

The *Follies* reopened on September 14, with a recovered Brice and with Bobby Clark replacing Bob Hope and Gypsy Rose Lee stepping in for Eve Arden. Evidently, they formed the new team that presented "I Can't Get Started." Josephine Baker, Gertrude Niesen, Hugh O'Connell, Harriet Hoctor, and the Nicholas Brothers also left the show, but a surprise replacement was Jane Pickins of the Pickins Sisters, a trio mostly heard on the air waves. A reviewer for the *The New York Times* noted she had learned "that lyrics sometimes make sense: often enough, at all events, to give the audience the benefit of the doubt." The show could not be called new, but the new materials were "generally up to the mark," including "Midnight Blue," by Edgar Leslie and Joe Burke and sung by Pickins, and "Harlem Waltz," "Ridin' the Rails," and "You Don't Love Right."[39]

Ira told Vernon in October, 1936 that he was "terribly happy about the *Follies*. Moss [Hart] wired it's one of the best revues he ever saw and who are we to refute him? So long as it continues to do over 28,000, it's the best revue ANYBODY ever saw."[40] The contract stated that no cuts in royalties would occur as long as the gross remained over $28,000 per week. But a short time later, Ira received a telegram from Kaufman, claiming that Vernon had agreed to a fifty percent cut in royalties. Vernon received a similar telegram stating that because of high overhead the show would have to close unless the authors agreed to the cut and claiming that Ira had agreed to it. A five or ten per cent cut was not unusual, but fifty per cent was catastrophic for those who relied on royalties for their livelihood. Because Vernon and Ira thought the other had agreed to the cut, each fell for the deception and accepted the new terms.[41]

On October 21, Vernon wrote to Ira about the swindle, labelling Kaufman "not only an ass, a horse's ass but also a cheap bitch" but insisting that "this was not a usual example of Duke tantrums, as I have given this matter much thought." He wondered why Ira had accepted the cut, "because by standing pat we would have won the battle." He was outraged that he still received a cut in royalties even though the gross for the second week was over $28,000. He apologized for his "Kauffmania," but had to present one more example of the man's ruthlessness. Will Irwin had four tunes in the show and was playing the piano at rehearsals to earn some extra money. Kaufman insisted that he rehearse for nothing, because he had given him a break by incorporating his songs. Irwin protested and was told he was a ungrateful son-of-a-bitch and would never work for the firm again. Apparently, there was little Vernon could do for Irwin, but his lawyer persuaded Kaufman to end the royalty swindle under threat that all of Vernon's materials would be withdrawn from the show. Kaufman also agreed that the show would be billed "Music Mostly by Vernon Duke."[42]

The show closed in New York on December 19, but in January 1937 it went on the road to several cities in the Midwest and South. After a few weeks in Chicago, it arrived in Cleveland in April and in Washington D.C. in May. Except for his high praise of the sketches featuring Bobby Clark and Fanny Brice, a reviewer for the local D.C. paper was less than positive: "Vernon Duke wrote the music of the 'Follies and Ira Gershwin the lyrics. And any one aware of what he has been humming the last few months will find very little that is familiar to the musical score of the show. 'Midnight Blue' is there, of course, and 'Moments of Moments' is rememberable (with more difficulty), but beyond that the words and music are not up to previous 'Follies.'"[43]

The troupe arrived in Evansville, Indiana on October 31. The local newspaper announced: "the *Ziegfeld Follies* will pull into town today in four large baggage cars and four Pullmans for a one-night showing in the Coliseum tomorrow night. Curtain is called for 8:15 o'clock."[44] The show received a moderately positive review from the local press: "It was honest entertainment. True, it lacked the dynamic punch that spells the difference between a hit and welded vaudeville, but for this stage-starved siding, it was welcome indeed....And though the patrons who were there evidently enjoyed it, they were up with the lights, and nary a curtain call."[45] By this time, the show may have lost its punch; it was certainly losing money. On November 11, Billie Burke cancelled a performance in Greensboro, North Carolina, ending the road tour.[46]

In its relative short run, thousands of people saw the *Ziegfeld Follies*, and presumably many of them, especially those in Boston and New York, stayed long enough to hear "I Can't Get Started." Because it was customary for the sheet music of some of the songs of a revue or musical play to be sold in the lobby where the show was being staged, many attendees must have perused or bought copies. At the Winter Garden, customers had their choice of "Island in the West Indies,"Words Without Music," "That Moment of Moments," and "I Can't Get Started."

I CAN'T GET STARTED

MRS. FLORENZ ZIEGFELD PRESENTS

ZIEGFELD FOLLIES

OF 1936

LYRICS BY
IRA GERSHWIN

MUSIC BY
VERNON DUKE

DEVISED AND STAGED BY
JOHN MURRAY ANDERSON

ISLAND IN THE WEST INDIES
WORDS WITHOUT MUSIC
THAT MOMENT OF MOMENTS
I CAN'T GET STARTED

CHAPPELL
L CO · INC ·
RKO BUILDING
ROCKEFELLER
CENTER·N·Y·C
CHAPPELL

As noted by Charles Hamm, from the time a song was published, "it then became fair game for performers, who according to the conventions of the genre were free to transform [it] in details of rhythm, harmony, melody, instrumentation, words, and even over all intent."[47] The transformation of "I Can't Get Started," began at a recording studio on January 18, 1936. That day Hal Kemp's sweet band recorded two songs: "That Moment of Moments" with a fine arrangement and sensitive vocalization by Bob Allen and an up-tempo version of "I Can't Get Started," with Skinnay Ennis singing it as a rhythm song in the lighthearted, whimsical way it was presented on Broadway. But this was just the beginning of the transformation. In February, John De Vries, sometime song writer and friend of jazz musicians, bought the sheet music at a performance of the revue. He dashed off to the "Famous Door" on 52nd Street and turned the music over to members of a jazz band booked into the club.[48]

They and increasing numbers of jazz artists found something unique in the song, something more than a typical upbeat show tune. It had depth and poignancy.

To hear the interpretations of the song discussed in the following Chapter Six, please consult http://renditions.website.

Chapter Six
Interpreting the Song:
From Bunny to Dizzy to Lennie

In early February 1936, singer Red McKenzie and guitarist Eddy Condon opened a jazz club in New York. *Variety* announced the event: "the team that made history in Chicago for OKeh records in 1927, are cutting riffs and licks at the Famous Door, NYC. This six piece outfit headlines Bunny Berigan, king of the Cornet, with Paul Ricci on tenor, Joe Bushkin on piano, Stoolmaker [sic] flapping the bass. . . .A bunch of musicians' musicians, McKenzie and Condon are bringing back the old days when the professionals flocked to the Door."[1]

The Famous Door got its name from its wooden door on which visitors scribbled their names. As recalled by Condon, the club "occupied the old quarters of the Onyx, with a downstairs room added. Billie Holiday, the singer, had preceded us, with Teddy Wilson on piano. . . .Lee Wiley, a girl from Oklahoma, dropped in to sing occasionally." The jam sessions held on Sundays were attended by some of the best jazz artists in the country. On one occasion, Bessie Smith stopped by and sang "Baby Won't You Please Come Home," "Nobody Knows You When You're Down and Out," and other songs associated with the great blues singer. Mildred Bailey was there, but wisely declined to sing, because "no one could follow Bessie." [2]

George Gershwin often frequented the Famous Door. On one occasion, while attending Hoagy Carmichael's wedding reception at the club, the band played his songs. As recalled by Joe Bushkin: "Gershwin—I can still see his face right in front of me—he couldn't believe what he was hearing. We did 'They Can't Take That Away From Me,' 'Strike up the Band,' ''S Wonderful.' We were swingin' that party backwards. He came over to me and said, 'By

God! I never heard my music played that way.' That was a hell of a compliment."[3] On another occasion, Kay Halle and George went to hear jazz violinist Stuff Smith and his band at the club. When the band had finished a swinging number, George asked Stuff what they had just played: "Why Mr. Gershwin, he chuckled, don't you recognize 'I Got Rhythm?'"[4]

Surprisingly, Condon had little to say about Bunny Berigan in his autobiography, but according to Berigan's biographer, "When Condon and McKenzie moved to the Famous Door in 1936, Berigan beat as the club's musical heart. Any recognition that Bunny had not already garnered within the music community quickly came his way now."[5] Born in Calumet County, Wisconsin on November 2, 1908, Rowland Bernart Berigan grew up in a musical family. His grandfather led the Fox Lake Community Band and got his grandson started on the violin at age six, but his first public appearance two years later was as a singer, accompanied by his mother on the piano. After the age of eleven, Bunny was playing the trumpet in his grandfather's fifteen member Fox Lake Juvenile Band. Two years later a band leader from a nearby town heard Bunny and hired him to play during the summer and on weekends. This experience led to an increasing number of jobs with dance bands, especially after he was sent to Madison to complete his high school education. But not all musicians who heard the young trumpet player, such as band leader Hal Kemp, were impressed. Greatness would come soon enough but only after an apprentice period of playing at fraternity parties and in stage bands.[6]

Bunny's technique improved and his musical education continued in New York, where in 1930 he met important people such as Jimmy and Tommy Dorsey and Hal Kemp who this time saw potential in the young man. When the Kemp band departed for Europe, Bunny was a member. Back in the United States, Bunny made nineteen recordings with the Kemp band before joining Fred Rich who led a house band for CBS. With other members of the band, Bunny cut dozens of sides and sang on one of them. The job, moreover, allowed him time to freelance, and between 1931 and 1936 he can be heard on hundreds of sides with such luminaries as the Dorsey Brothers, saxophonists Frank Trumbauer and Bud Freeman, guitarist Dick McDonough, drummer Ray Bauduc and clarinetists Artie Shaw and Benny Goodman. After touring with Goodman, Bunny returned to the CBS orchestra and continued to freelance.[7]

At the Famous Door, Berigan took possession of "I Can't Get Started," turning a rhythm song into a ballad. As recalled by George Frazier, "He used to play it back in the vagrant nights when he and Red McKenzie had a hole-in-the-wall on West 52d street that was charitably called a night club." That the two of them used to drink up the slim profits never bothered them because jazz was all that they cared about. Jack Teagarden often dropped by for a night-cap or two and they would play the blues for a half hour solid:

> AND THEN BUNNY would get up on the platform and raise his horn to his lips. The notes would swell across the room in all their rugged masculinity and it would be 'Can't Get Started.' That was a majestic thing—the most impassioned torch song you ever heard. It was a concerto for trumpet. Later on, it got onto a record, of course, and every kid from Brunswick, Me., to Palo Alto, Calif., and back to New Haven, Ct., could hum it to you and doubtless did. Which shouldn't have disturbed anyone, because it has all the man's virtues and none of his defects. It has his magnificent sense of construction. It has a beginning, a middle, and an end. It tells a story, and it tells it in that massive, brooding style, building note by note into one of the greatest solos on or off records. It has dignity and as long as the record of it is to be heard, no one can dismiss jazz as specious.[8]

Red McKenzie and his Rhythm Kings recorded "I Can't Get Started" on April 3, 1936. Berigan begins with a solo that sticks to the melody and takes the song to the bridge. A tenor saxophonist stays with melody to the end of the bridge. Bunny returns and solos to the end of the first chorus. The second chorus consists of a vocal by McKenzie, who, in his high baritone rather polished voice, a voice good enough for Paul Whiteman to later hire him, gives a good account of himself. After a pianist plays the bridge, Berigan returns and stays with the melody until the rest of the ensemble enters to bring the song to an end. Although a fine rendition, Berigan was limited to playing only the melody.

On April 13, he recorded the song as "Bunny Berigan and his Boys." Only ten days separated the two recordings, and the arrangement of the second borrows much from the first. Supposedly, the personnel on the second recording differed from those on the first, but the sound of the instruments and the fill-ins are so similar that it is difficult to accept this view. Although Artie Shaw failed to mention the session in his autobiography, apparently he was on clarinet, with Forrest Crawford on tenor sax, Joe Bushkin on the piano, Dave Tough on drums, and Mort Stuhlmaker on bass.

Jazz historian and trumpet player Richard M. Sudhalter wrote: "After a thoughtful opening tutti, Berigan sings a chorus in his high light voice, his fast vibrato lending a sense of vulnerability. Crawford's tenor takes eight bars in a subdued ballad mood, and then it's all Bunny, playing at a bravura peak. Moving easily throughout the entire range of his horn, he climbs at the outset to a titanic high concert Db and Eb, only to plunge near the end to four broad-tone sotto voce bars, before a final climactic ascent."[9] Gunther Schuller also has high praise for this rendition: "a beautiful performance, quite original in its design and proportions: eight bars of Berigan theme, a Berigan vocal, a trumpet cadenza, and the final majestic high-register peroration." Schuller found the musicians "virtually perfect," especially Artie Shaw's sympathetic clarinet obbligato fill-ins and Joe Bushkins's lacy webs of enveloping piano garlands."[10] The rendition was immediately recognized as something special. Gordon Wright of *Metronome* considered it one of the best recordings of it 1936: "Inspirational Berigan blowing and singing of his favorite song, plus great Dave Tough drums and Forest Crawford tenor sax."[11]

In 1937 Berigan made another recording of "I Can't Get Started." Although the 1936 rendition can stand on its own as excellent jazz, the new version has received most of the attention, and in a relatively short time became one of the most recognizable of all jazz solos. Recorded as "Bunny Berigan and his Orchestra," it consisted of a trombone, three trumpets, three saxophones, guitar, bass, and drums. Unlike the 1936 recording, this one was recorded on a twelve-inch disk and was issued in a four-record set called *A Symposium of Swing*. The song lasted nearly five minutes, two minutes longer than the first version. This rendition drew heavily from the previous one, including the vocal, cadenza, and finale, but to introduce the piece another cadenza was added. Played rubato on four sustained chords—C, B7, Dm, and G7s, the cadenza, observed Schuller, "Rather than seeming gratuitous or redundant, somehow it adds to the grandeur of the performance." Although it has been compared to Louis Armstrong's "West End Blues," the cadenza should be seen more as "a nobel first extension of it."[12]

Robert Dupuis has analyzed the chorus: "The next eight measures are taken aloft, exposed to the rarefied air of Bunny's upper register, where he sculpts a melody now become his own, rising to a high F, and punctuated with three piercing E-flats. All this is played without sacrifice of tonal quality or size. The emotional level peaks as well. Immediately then he drops down nearly three octaves to his low G, restarting the theme for the last time in his voluptuous low register, before moving to a rich vibrant, mid-range E-flat in preparing for the finale." To end the rendition, "Bunny arrives at the high B-flat, invests it with a rich vibrato, and holds it. Now, instead of moving up, Bunny drops to a G, before soaring to hold the magnificent final E-flat. The dramatic and emotional impact are searing."[13]

This solo has received such high praise from musicians, critics, and historians that it is surprising, indeed refreshing, that

there is a contrarian out there—Richard Sudhalter—who clearly favors the 1936 version. Regarding the 1937 rendition, he wrote: "Bunny's way of playing the song had crystallized into a routine, as formalized and polished as a trumpet concerto; any variation was at best a matter of detail." Whereas the earlier version "seemed casual, almost tossed off, in its brilliance, the twelve-inch 1937 reading exudes as aura of gravitas, a self conscious high seriousness." It is "a grand gesture, not without a certain rather disquieting stridency."[14]

Another recording of the song, a so-called dub version, was issued in 1937 on a ten-inch record. Eliminated were the cadenzas and all the creativity of the first two recordings.

In both his 1936 and 1937 versions, Berigan interjects his singing, so that it becomes another solo, and thus is an integral part of the performance. This was a common practice at the time. But two jazz historians took issue with the inclusion. James Lincoln Collier regretted that he sang on the recording, and Ted Gioia found Berrigan's singing "less impressive" than his playing but acknowledged that it probably contributed to the sales of the record.[15] Clearly the quality of his voice does not hold up in comparison to Red McKenzie's, but as Dupuis has pointed out, "Any objective evaluation of Bunny's singing voice would surely conclude that it possesses significant defects. It is high-pitched and distinctly throaty. . . .Whereas his trumpet tone and vibrato are controlled, deep, and enveloping, his voice is often quavery, shallow, and vapid. Yet somehow—at least with this song—it works." As Dupuis correctly observed, the voices of many singers, such as Johnny Mercer and Mel Tormé (I would add Louis Armstrong and Jack Teagarden), would not "withstand careful scrutiny. But they are musical singers and they do communicate! And so does Bunny."[16]

Gunther Schuller concurred:

> As it turned out, his superb musicianship
> and taste more than compensated for the lack of a
> trained or a natural voice. One is surprised at first
> by the timbre of the voice, a light tenor quality in a
> baritone range. It is tender, soft-spoken, with a fast
> little vibrato that has its own peculiar attractiveness.
> Moreover his singing is relaxed and rhythmically
> free—like his middle register ballad trumpet-
> playing—and totally unpretentious. But I think
> that what ultimately fascinates us, what enables
> us to hear this vocal rendition. . .hundreds of times
> without tiring of it, is that Berigan's singing is a kind
> of window into his soul. The voice—particularly
> the "amateur" voice—is the most personal of all
> instruments, of course, and it is virtually impossible
> to hide anything behind it, for it exposes all. And
> what we hear in Berigan's voice—refracted through
> Vernon Duke's poignant melody and Ira Geshwin's
> bittersweet lyrics—is his human vulnerability, his
> frailty.[17]

Put another way, Berigan found in the lyric not the
exaggerations of a guy claiming entitlement to the woman he
was pursuing as in the *Follies* but the sufferings of a man in love.
Although his trumpet solo remains his greatest contribution to jazz,
Bunny's vocalization advertised to many that the song could be—
indeed should be—sung as a ballad.

Ever attuned to the jazz scene, Vernon Duke wrote to Ira
Gershwin in October, joking "that he just can't get started in NY"
but noting that "you'll be happy to know that there are two new
records of that tune on the market—one on Brunswick, the other
a swing classic 12 inch job on Victor."[18] The Brunswick recording
refers to the Hal Kemp version, the Victor to the second Berigan
recording.

All the trumpet players of the late 1930s and early 1940s deferred recording the song. On one occasion, Louis Armstrong told a friend you do not touch that one; it belongs to Bunny. When asked in an interview with *Down Beat* in 1941 who were his favorite trumpet players, Armstrong said: "first I'll name my boy Bunny Berigan. Now there's a boy I've always admired for his tone, soul, technique, his sense of phrasing and all. To me, Bunny can't do no wrong in music."[19]

In ill health from his prodigious consumption of liquor, Bunny was confined to a Pennsylvania hospital for eighteen days in April and May of 1942 with pneumonia. But soon he was booked into the Palomar Ballroom in Norfolk, Virginia. He announced to the audience that he had "a lot of requests to play our theme song, I Can't Get Started. Well, you'll have to pardon me, but I just got out of the hospital a few weeks ago, and I'm not feeling up to par. Now, I'll tell you what I'll do. I'll try to play it for you." He died on June 2, 1942.[20]

Because the lyric to "I Can't Get Started" was designed for a male singer, it is not surprising that males Skinnay Ennis, Red McKenzie, and Bunny Berigan were the first to record vocals of the song. Whether that situation had any thing to do with Billie Holiday's decision to record the song is not known, but one would like to think it did. To many, Billie Holiday needs no introduction, but a short biography will bring her life to the time of her recording. Born in Baltimore, Maryland on April 7 or 17, 1915, Eleanora Holiday was the offspring of musician Clarence Holiday and Sadie Fagan. First deserted by her father and later dumped by her mother onto her maternal grandparents, Billie grew up lonely and often hungry. Raped at age ten, she was sent to a home for wayward girls, the punishment for "enticing" her abuser. Although her sentence was to run until her twenty-first birthday, she was released earlier, and about 1927 rejoined her mother in Long Branch, New Jersey. Her job as a maid did not last very long, and her mother sent her to a madam in Harlem where she was employed for the next two years as a prostitute. But on one occasion, after refusing to serve a well-connected customer with the police, she was arrested for prostitution and spent four months in jail. After her release she served a pimp for a time before taking a waitressing job on Long Island where she also sang at the local Elks Club. Reunited with her mother in Harlem, she extorted money from her long-lost and indifferent father who was playing guitar with the Fletcher Henderson orchestra. She promised to never call him "daddy" in public in exchange for money to pay the rent.[21]

Her first full-time singing job was at the The Log Cabin in New York City and in November 1933, she cut her first records with a combo led by Benny Goodman. Other engagements followed and soon she became well known to the jazz crowd. She was booked into the Apollo Theater in April 1935, and in July she joined Teddy Wilson, Benny Goodman, Roy Eldridge, Ben Webster and others in a recording session. In these sessions, she sang as another member of an ensemble, sharing time with the instrumentalists. Her engagement at the Famous Door in September with Teddy Wilson, however, did not go well. The audience that came to hear the main attraction, George Brunies and his New Orleans-style group, was not that impressed with her subtle singing, and she quit after four days. An engagement at Chicago's Grand Terrance Cafe in the summer of 1936 also led to a firing—for singing too slowly. Tours with the Count Basie big band in 1937 and with Artie Shaw's all white band the following year led to experiences she could have done without. She loved singing for Basie, but was fired for inconsistent performances. While touring with Shaw in the South and in the North she experienced racial prejudice, and the management of band prohibited her from singing on Shaw's fifteen minute radio broadcast because she was too artistic. Helen Forrest performed the numbers as they were written. [22]

In September 1938, she recorded "I Can't Get Started" under "Billie Holiday and Her Orchestra." The personnel included Lester Young on tenor sax; "Countess" Margaret "Queenie" Johnson, piano; Freddie Green, guitar; Walter Page, string bass; and Jo Jones drums. After a brief introduction by Young, she sings through the first chorus, and then Young takes the song to the bridge. Billie returns and finishes the song. Unlike her earlier recordings, when she shared the song with the instrumentalists, on this one she takes up most of the time. According to jazz historian Gary Giddins, it was about this time "her recordings lost much of their impulsive, huddling spontaneity. The singer became the star, not just one of the gang singing one chorus among many, but the performer around whom the entire recording was built."[23]

Her interpretation has produced both positive and critical comments. Melvin Maddocks noted how she played with the lyric. "But what good does it do" became "Baby, but what good does it do," "thus adding an extra dimension of musical and emotional meaning." Moreover, she also combined two moods: "'You're so supreme' is all full-lipped tenderness. 'I've been consulted by Franklin D,' gets delivered by the salty streetwise Billie out of the side of her mouth, as it were. And in triumph of heart over smart, she subdues into a lovely gentleness the chic word-playing rhymes: 'When first we met, how you elated me! Pet, you devastated me!'"[24] Interestingly, while the male vocalists remained mostly faithful to the sheet music version of the lyric, most of Holiday's lyric came from the original *Follies,'* version, although she changed "Greta Garbo's asked me to tea" to "Robert Taylor had me to tea."

Gunther Schuller had no problem with what Holiday did with the lyric. What she did with the melody, however, bothered him: "were it not for the stated title and the lyrics one would not recognize it as Vernon Duke's famous song. Granted that Billie on many occasions improved certain songs with her improvised amendments. But one wonders what motivated her to flatten out one of the finest tunes of the decade into something much less imaginative than Vernon Duke's original."[25]

Maddocks' and Schuller's opinions of the song deserve challenging. I think Maddocks stretches things beyond credulity when he claims that adding "baby" to the lyrics "adds an extra dimension of musical and emotional meaning." He even admitted that only after listening to the song two or three times did this become apparent. One wonders what a fourth time would have produced. And to claim, as Schuller has done, that without knowing the title one could not recognize the song simply does not hold.

Whether one likes or dislikes Holiday's interpretation, the song is recognizable.

To be strongly noted, however, is that Schuller has much to say that is positive about Holiday's singing, and he also has much to say about the songs she and other vocalists chose to sing. Between 1935 and 1938 over a hundred songs were composed, so some of them had to be of high quality, but "it is fashionable for the jazz critics to trash the songs and their composers (with the exception of Gershwin, of course, and a few beknighted [sic] others), while praising the jazz musicians for elevating the allegedly wretched material to such sublime heights. But can it really have been all that bad?" If improvisation is a priori better than the song on which it is based, then those who improvise always improve the song. "Neither Billie Holiday's hundreds of recordings nor those of thousands of other jazz artists can even remotely begin to demonstrate such an assumption."[26]

Surprisingly, a more daring rendition of "I Can't Get Started" was offered by cabaret-singer Hildegarde, who on April 17, 1939 was featured in and on the cover of *Life Magazine*. Described as "a new star of radio and the brightest star rising over television's horizon," she was "good on radio because she has a catchy voice. She is even better on television because she is blond, glamorous . . . , has a nice figure and a flexible face." Unmarried and twenty-seven years old, "Hildegard works hard on her songs. When she sings well, she says she feels mice run up and down her legs."[27]

Often billed as the "Incomparable Hildegarde," she was especially popular during the 1930s and 40s, when she performed at plush supper clubs and cabarets. Born as Loretta Sell in Wisconsin, she studied music at Marquette University for a time before becoming a member of a vaudeville troupe for two seasons and a piano accompanist to various performers for two years. She plugged songs for Irving Berlin, sang in clubs in London and Paris, and acted in several British movies and revues. Thus, when she appeared on the cover of *Life*, Hildegard had achieved considerable fame.[28]

Hildegarde's glamour and reputation (she had numerous romances and never married) may have entered into Vernon Duke's decision to record with her. In his autobiography, he called her "a tantalizing wholesome Milwaukee 'bachfisch'" and mentioned that her sponsor suggested that he, she, and her pianist, Leo Kahn, do an album of his songs. Duke was happy with the result: "It turned out a good album (Decca)—Dave Kapp supervising shrewdly, Hildegarde singing continentally and Leo and I playing 'a lot of piano.'"[29] Indeed, the dissonance in their solo on "I Can't Get Started" was seldom heard in popular records. And the feminization of part of the lyric adds another dimension to the song. She ends the verse with "Super girl is finally lost in the world." In one part of the chorus she sings "Marlene Dietrich copied my hat" and on another "Glamor girls follow my style." Included in the three-record album are "April in Paris," "Now," "Suddenly," "I Cling to You," and "What is There to Say?" all of which allow Vernon to demonstrate his masterly piano concepts and Hildegarde to express her emotional sensitivity.

Cabaret singer Bobby Short admitted in an interview with Max Wilk that until he heard Vernon accompanying Hildegarde one night, he never cared much for the Bunny Berigan version of

Hildegarde in an Album of Songs by Vernon Duke, Decca 149, 23M Series

"I Can't Get Started," "as famous as it was, and as much fun as it was to hear." To him it "never really captured the essence of the musicality that Duke had applied to the melody of that song."[30]

By 1940 the song probably had been added to the stock arrangements of many sweet bands.   It can easily be played as a dance number and sung in a safe and conventional way. That year, Ginny Simms, the vocalist of the Kay Kyser sweet band, recorded "I Can't Get Started." Born in San Antonio, Texas in 1913 but educated at Fresno State Teachers College in California, Simms began singing in a trio with two members of her sorority. After a stint with the Tommy Gerun band, she joined Kyser's band in 1934 and appeared in films with Kyser and in *Night and Day*, the very fictional biography of Cole Porter, starring Cary Grant and Alexis Smith. Simms recorded "I Can't Get Started" under her name but was backed up by members of Kyser's orchestra.[31]

Supported by a rhythm guitar, unobtrusive drums, and a clarinet, she sings the first chorus. The full band comes in with the second chorus and is a bit ponderous; Simms returns with the

bridge, stays with the melody, and sings with some feeling. The arrangement is fairly representative of the popular big band style of the 1940s. Of all the vocalists who sang in Kyser's band through the years, Mel Tormé considered Simms one of the best.[32]

The three female versions of the song allow us to appreciate and compare the vocal interpretations the song underwent in just a few short years. A jazz, cabaret, and big band singer would have different objectives in recording the song. Holiday probably understood that her rendition would appeal mainly to her followers. With a rather conventional arrangement backing her up, Simms sought to reach a broader audience and probably did. Because of the complexity of their arrangement, Hildegrade and Duke perhaps freed themselves from any illusions about the commercial possibilities of their rendition and thus recorded it and the other songs just for the love of it. Of the three vocalists, she was the only one to include the verse to "I Can't Get Started." Obviously exhibiting bias and probably committing heresy, I consider her recording with Duke and Kahn superior to Holiday's with Lester Young.

The instrumental renditions offered by two of the greatest jazz pianists also calls for comparison. Art Tatum and Teddy Wilson recorded "I Can't Get Started" a few years apart, Art in 1938, Teddy in 1941. Their solos clearly place them within the Swing Era and demonstrate why they are two of the most easily recognizable pianists in all of jazz.

Born in Toledo, Ohio on October 13, 1909, to Art and Mildred Tatum, a first generation of black South Carolinians born free, Art Tatum, Jr. grew up in a less than affluent household but in an economically and socially stable one. The musical talents of Art Junior were discovered early, and because of an eyesight disability he spent much of his time at the piano. After giving him rudimentary lessons, his mother hired a teacher, and he learned to read music in Braille. After attending two schools for the handicapped, where he studied the violin and guitar, he was placed in the Toledo School of Music. Although encouraged to study classical music, for which he never lost his love, Art drifted towards jazz and at sixteen was playing with local dance bands until joining first the Speed Webb and then the Milton Senior bands. Work at local clubs refined his playing as did his gig with the Radio WSPD, where he played at interludes. Soon he got his own fifteen minute show which was picked up by NBC Blue network and broadcast nationally.[33]

He then decided to try his luck in New York. He teamed up with Adelaide Hall at the Lafayette Theater and later at the Palace and cut four records with her. In 1933 he recorded solo four more songs: "St. Louis Blues," "Tiger Rag," "Tea for Two," and "Sophisticated Lady."[34] He also played at George Gershwin's apartment. "Tatum amazed the guests with his "remarkable runs, embroideries, counter-figures and passage playing," recalled Oscar Levant. The composer pianist/composer Leopold Godowsky, however, was bored after about twenty minutes of an hour-and-a-half concert.[35]

Tatum's 1933 records did not attract much attention, and the eighteen he cut in 1934 did not lead to employment. He returned to the Midwest, where he found work playing first in a Cleveland joint called the "Greasy Spoon" and later in the "Three Deuces" in Chicago. In Los Angeles in 1936, he was greatly appreciated and was even a guest on the Bing Crosby radio show.[36] At a night club, George Gershwin, Oscar Levant, and other enthusiasts witnessed Tatum's genius: "To George's great joy," recalled Levant, "Tatum played virtually the equivalent of Beethoven's thirty-two variations on his tune 'Liza.' Then George asked for more."[37] Tatum returned to the "Three Deuces" and then in 1938 moved to New York for an engagement at the "Famous Door," where Teddy Wilson sometimes played.[38]

Theodore Shaw Wilson was born in Austin Texas on November 24, 1912 to parents who taught at Samuel Huston College. They moved to Tuskegee, Alabama, where James Wilson became head of the English department and his mother, Augustus, a librarian, found employment at the Tuskegee Institute, the school founded by Booker T. Washington for African Americans. Teddy and his older brother received an early education in music. And in high school, Teddy first played the oboe and E flat clarinet and then the piano. His fascination with jazz came from listening to recordings of Bix Beiderbecke, Frank Trumbauer, King Oliver, Earl Hines, Fats Waller, Louis Armstrong, and others. In the late 1920s, Teddy spent part of his vacations in Detroit, where he heard McKinney's Cotton Pickers and the Fletcher Henderson orchestra.[39]

His decision to become a full-time musician, which clashed with his mother's desire he receive a higher education, came after one year at Talladega College. There, however, he got an elementary musical education and a lifelong passion for classical music. It was then off to Detroit where he picked up gigs in clubs until joining the Speed Webb band, which toured the country's heartland during 1929 and 1930. He left Webb the following year to join a band in Toledo, Ohio led by Milton Senior. He replaced Art Tatum who had taken a job at a radio station. But at the station Teddy sometimes played duets with Art, and together they would hit the hot spots around town. At different venues, Teddy often asked Art to replay his trademark runs at a slow tempo so he could learn the notes and fingering. Wilson's indebtedness to Tatum can clearly be heard in his playing, but he also acknowledged Earl Hines and Fats Waller as important influences. In time he refined a sophisticated style of his own.[40]

After the Milton Senior band folded, Teddy remained in Chicago and married pianist Irene Armstrong. He found work around town, and beginning in early 1933 toured with Louis Armstrong. Back in Chicago, he again worked in clubs until "discovered" by promoter John Hammond who offered him a job in New York. There, he recorded with alto saxophonist Benny Carter and his "Chocolate Dandies." After the Carter band folded, Teddy joined the Willie Brant band which included drummer Cozy Cole, tenor saxophonist Ben Webster, and later Benny Carter. During his time with the band, Teddy would sit in with musicians, such as Bunny Berigan, at the Famous Door. He also agreed to make a series of small-group recordings for John Hammond. Consisting of whomever was in town, the recordings featured many of the great jazz musicians of the time, including Billie Holiday.[41]

Teddy also met Benny Goodman, with whom he recorded in 1934. Two years later he joined the Goodman big band, although he only appeared with Benny and drummer Gene Krupa between sets. And when vibraphonist Lionel Hampton was added, a quartet was formed that made recording history. Wilson stayed with Goodman until 1939, when he formed his own band and obtained the freedom to record with whomever he wanted.[42]

Because Teddy and Art were contemporaries and pianists who often recorded solo, Gunther Schuller has offered a brief comparison of their styles:

> It is a measure of Wilson and Tatum's greatness that, although they were weaned on many of the same musical sources—Hines, Jelly Roll Morton, classical piano literature—they developed totally individual idioms. A comparison of the two pianists' musical/stylistic conceptions reveals clearly how distinct and diverse were their musical personalities. If there is one domain where these differences are most pronounced it is in the realm of harmony. Whereas Tatum's ear and temperament compelled him to push constantly to the permissible outer limits of the harmonic vocabulary, Wilson was—to the end—harmonically a staunch conservative. Tatum's harmonic energy is unbounded, whereas Wilson's stays very clearly within well-defined limits. Moreover, Tatum's emphasis on harmonic exploration leads him to sacrifice melodic interest, and often rhythmic as well; whereas, of course, Wilson's emphasis on melody and rhythm compels him to sacrifice harmonic invention.[43]

Foregoing the verse, Tatum swings "I Can't Get Started" at a moderate tempo, but repeatedly breaks the rhythm, as he was wont to do, with long descending arpeggios. Also without the verse, Wilson first plays the song rubato until the second chorus which he swings in 4/4 time. Wilson keeps his arpeggios to a minimum, and plays in a relaxed way as if he were interpreting the lyrics. Because Tatum plays the song in such a dynamic way, it is hard to imagine the lyrics were ever under consideration. Moreover, clearly discernible in each rendition are techniques that exemplify Schuller's generalizations about their playing: "Tatum's arpeggios invariably are descending, zooming downward like an arrow, usually encompassing the entire range of the piano from the highest tinkling octave to the lowest forceful bass notes. Wilson's arpeggios, on the other hand, more often than not are both descending and ascending, swooping down and up, usually back to the point of origin."[44] Seldom in the history of recorded jazz are we able to appreciate two musicians—in this case pianists—of similar musical influences playing the same song solo a few years apart.

A year after Wilson's interpretation, the great tenor saxophonist Lester Young also recorded the song, thus ensuring that jazz would continue to play a major role in spreading its appeal. Young was born in Woodville, Mississippi on August 27, 1909, but spent his first ten years at Algiers, across the Mississippi River from New Orleans, where he often went to hear the street bands. From his father, he learned to play trumpet, alto saxophone, violin, and drums. After touring with his father's band, first as its drummer and then as a saxophonist, he quit and settled in Salina, Kansas where in 1928 he joined the Art Bronson band, having been encouraged to switch to the tenor saxophone by the bandleader. After stints with various bands, including those led by Bennie Moten, Count Basie, Fletcher Henderson, Andy Kirk, and others, he rejoined Basie with whom he remained until December 1940. He moved to Los Angeles the following year and formed a band with his brother.[45]

On July 15, 1942, Young cut four sides. He was accompanied by Red Callender on bass and Nat "King" Cole, a superb jazz pianist before he became a well-known pop singer. Gunther Schuller calls the collaboration in which "Body and Soul" was also recorded as "historic." Having left the Basie band, he freed himself from a "riff-oriented swinger, playing mostly for dances, into a romantic ballad player, appearing as a 'soloist' at clubs and concerts. Lester's straightforward approach to 'I Can't Get Started' is intriguingly complemented by Cole's ornate piano style, harmonically more adventurous and conceptually more linear than, say, either Teddy Wilson's or Basie's—Lester's primary accompanists up until then."[46]

The linearity of Young's playing is explained by Donald L. Maggin: "Instead of moving up and down each chord vertically, he would create an independent melodic line that he fashioned to fit over the chords, a horizontal flow of notes that he made sure would agree with what the chordal harmony was doing. . . .Young would speak in musical sentences of varying lengths as he perfected a narrative style rooted in the storytelling southwestern blues culture that nurtured him."[47] His storytelling suggests he knew the lyric of "I Can't Get Started."

The Lester Young recording was one of the last to be released commercially in 1942. The United States had entered World War II at the end of the previous year and was quickly changing to a war economy. Products and supplies were diverted to the war-related industries. People entered the military or found new jobs. That these social and economic changes would have a great impact on musicians is hardly surprising. What is surprising, however, is that The American Federation of Musicians would call a strike that year over royalty payments. It began on August 1 and forbade its members to record with any recording company.[48]

Edward A. Wolpin of Chappell & Company wrote to Ira Gershwin in early 1943 about the strike and the future of "I Can't Get Started." He attached a list of the companies that had recorded the song and mentioned his promise to them that he would begin plugging the song if they released their best recordings when the strike ended." He asked Ira "to make many changes in the lyric in order to make this song COMMERICAL. The new edition will be a popular one and the more commercial you make it the better chance we have of establishing it as a hit song."[49]

The strike continued, but artists could perform in concerts, on radio programs, and they could cut Victory Disks, or V-Disks, for distribution to the armed forces but not for sale to the general public. Recording sessions were held in studios, on sound stages, in night clubs, and on military bases from coast to coast, and more than eight million V-disks were recorded and distributed. Many prominent pop and jazz artists participated in the program. For example, in 1943 pianist Carmen Cavallaro cut a V-Disk that included "I Can't Get Started."   A student of the classical piano for much of his youth, in the 1930s he joined the sweet bands of Al Kavelin, Rudy Vallee and Abe Lyman.   In 1944 he formed his own orchestra, and recorded nearly a dozen songs on V-Disks.[50]

An announcer or artist would often introduced a song on a V-Disk. In this case, it was Cavallaro's young daughter, Delores. Carmen plays a medley of four songs that concludes with "I Can't Get Started." The first chorus is presented up tempo, the melody ornamented with cascading arpeggios. He plays the second chorus in double time, as if to demonstrate   that he too can play jazz (I suspect he had heard the Wilson and Tatum versions). The melody is now covered with "jazzy" runs and phrases, but they seem composed and rehearsed. He ends at the bridge and returns to the tempo of the first chorus. Cavallaro's version may sound today exceedingly lush, if not corny, but it probably gave the service men and women of World War II the kind of nostalgic music they longed for.

Far from corny is the rendition Kay Starr cut with the Charlie Barnet orchestra. To many old-timers she is remembered for her 1950s hits such as "Wheel of Fortune" and "Bonaparte's Retreat." But like many of the pop singers of the 1950s, she honed her craft as a member of big bands during the 1940s. Born Katherine LaVerne Starks of an Iroquois father and a part Indian mother in Dougherty, Oklahoma on July 21, 1922, she demonstrated a singing talent at an early age, and after the family moved to Dallas she won talent competitions. The family then moved to Memphis, Tennessee, where Katherine got jobs singing pop and country songs and where the family name was changed to Starr. At fifteen she joined the Joe Venuti orchestra. After the Venuti band broke up in 1942, she had brief stints with Bob Crosby and Glenn Miller, with whom she made her first two recordings. For a time while In Los Angeles, she sang with the Wingy Manone band.[51]

From 1943 to 1946, she was with the great Barnet orchestra, and in September of the latter year recorded "I Can't Get Started" on a V-Disk. With a flurry, the band announces a song is forthcoming. We hear applause, followed by an introduction by Barnet: "Thank you very much. Being a very naive sort of fellow, I can't quite figure out why the folks at V-Disks get so many requests from soldiers for girl singers. Of course when I see someone as attractive as Kay Starr, I catch on a bit quicker. I think you will too, when you hear Kay Starr sing the song whose lyrics and melody are so popular with G.I's., 'I Can't Get Started with You.'" As a big-band vocalist, she probably sang the song much the same way each time, but her slightly blues-inflected, Billie Holiday-influenced interpretation seems remarkably fresh. Will Friedwald wrote in *Jazz Singing* that "Starr isn't blues-ish. Starr isn't blues-y. She is thoroughly blue. Bluer, in fact, that you'd think any white woman has a right to be."[52] According to Holiday's biographer, Billie considered Starr the only white vocalist who could sing the blues.[53]

The musicians' strike ended on November 11, 1944 but without the royalty issue being resolved. The following year tenor saxophonist Ben Webster recorded "I Can't Get Started" with the Teddy Wilson Sextet. Webster, like Lester Young, was born in 1909 and on the 27th of a month, except it was March. Before turning to the alto saxophone, he studied violin and piano, and, ironically, joined the band led by Young's father, who helped him learn to read music. Ben and Lester, both in their early twenties, became good friends, and they often practiced together. Ben remained with the Young band for nine months before joining the Eugene Coy Black Aces and devoting his musical life to the tenor saxophone. And like Lester, he too spent time with Benny Moten, Andy Kirk, and Fetcher Henderson. From 1940 to 1943, he was a member of the Duke Ellington orchestra and was featured on several recordings. He quit the orchestra over a pay dispute, and worked with small groups in Chicago and at clubs on 52nd Street in New York City.[54]

Guitarist Al Casey's chordal introduction sets the tone. Webster takes over and except for a recognizable note here and there floats above the melody. Trumpeter Buck Clayton comes in (sounding at bit like Bunny) and follows the melody until Wilson fashions a beautiful solo. Clayton returns and carries the melody to the conclusion with Webster weaving a counter melody in the background. Of this recording John Chilton wrote: "There is no sense of competition in Webster's splendid performance, not a touch of the tension that characterizes the famous Berigan solo. Webster is at the opposite pole—relaxed, confident, sounding as though he feels he can get started."[55] Because of the superb musicianship of the players, their flawless coordination in the execution of the song, and their obvious pride in playing their style of music, the recording is close to perfect. Recorded about the time the "Swing Era" was coming to an end, it is one of the best examples of small-group jazz of that period.

Lee Wiley was one of the best jazz singers of that era, but she also had popular appeal. Born in Oklahoma on in 1910, she claimed to be part Native American. As a teenager, she ran away from home to Chicago and then to New York where she became a member of the Leo Reisman orchestra. During the early 1930s, she was featured on several radio programs, and later in the decade and into the next she became the first vocalist to systematically link jazz with the musical theater. In 1939 and 1940 she issued albums of the songs of Cole Porter, Rodgers and Hart, and Ira and George Gershwin in which she was supported by jazz musicians such as Max Kaminsky, Joe Bushkin, Pee Wee Russell, Bud Freeman, Fats Waller and Bunny Berigan. In 1944 she married pianist Jess Stacy and toured with his big band.[56]

As noted by music critic John S. Wilson, her "voice—warm and easy and with a wide vibrato—was often remarked on for its erotic effect. Such comments were invariably associated with admiration for her ability to choose superior material and to deliver it with unusual sensitivity." On one occasion she insisted she did not sing   jazz: "I just sing. The only vocal trick I've ever done is putting in the vibrato and taking it out. I don't believe in vocal gimmickry and I had never had the commercial instincts to concentrate on visual mannerisms." If she did not like something, she would not do it.[57] Will Friedwald's view that Wiley "extends no defenses, no walls, no barriers between her heart and her audience" is remarkably perceptive.[58] Mel Tormé considered her "a great delineator of verses. . . .She would sing these 'set-ups' rubato, going into tempo at the chorus. Consequently, the songs were complete, the meaning of the lyrics clear. In this respect, she was a major contributor to the inventory of the popular song and its performance on record and in person."[59]

On February 10, 1945, in a radio broadcast from the Broadway Ritz Theater, she sang "I Can't Get Started," unfortunately without the verse, but only as a jazz singer could. Backed up by a trio with Stacy on piano, her slightly blues inflections when she emotes "But I Can't Get Started with You" adds poignancy to the song. Unlike many singers, Wiley made her statements by understating. Late the following year, supported by an all-star jazz band, she sang only Gershwin songs at a Town Hall concert.[60]

Although Wiley would continue to sing for many more years, the "Swing Era," was winding down, forcing many musicians to adapt or find new ways of making a living. But the Artie Shaw 1945 recording of "I Can't Get Started" suggests that the big band boys were not yet through, that they still had some life in them. Unfortunately, Shaw has emerged in retrospect as someone larger than life—not just because of his musicianship, which was outstanding, but because of his episodes off the bandstand and after his retirement from music. As Gunther Schuller put it, "The anomalies in Shaw's public career, fully justifying the terms 'enigmatic' and 'contradictory,' are so numerous and complex as to make objective evaluation of his work as a musical artist a formidable task."[61] Shaw's autobiography, *The Trouble with Cinderella*, although fascinating reading, is as much about his personal struggles as it is about his musical contributions.

On May 23, 1910, Arthur Arshawsky was born in the Lower Side of New York but grew up in New Haven, Connecticut. At an early age he demonstrated his musical abilities first on the ukulele and then on the saxophone. At fifteen he left home to become a professional musician. After working with a several traveling bands, he arrived in New York where he found work with local band leaders, including trumpeter Red Nichols. In 1934 he retired from music to run a farm in Pennsylvania. But he returned to New York and formed a small group consisting of clarinet (to which he had switched) strings and a rhythm section. The hit it made at a concert at the Imperial Theater in New York in May 1936 led to financial support that allowed him to organize a big band with strings, but its existence was short lived. Shaw then formed a conventional big band which debuted in Boston in April 1937. The recording of "Begin the Beguine" in 1938 brought fame to Shaw and his orchestra. Two years later with "Frenesi" he had another hit. Never happy with the music business, he disbanded his band in 1939 but formed a new one the following year and began recording with members of that group called the "Gramercy Five." During World War II he served in the Navy and led a service band that toured throughout the Pacific. He was discharged in 1944 and organized another big band.[62]

Many of those analyzing his music include Schuller: "By 1939 Shaw had progressed from a proficient imitator of Benny Goodman to a real master of the clarinet, virtually incomparable in the beauty of his tone and unique in his flawless control of the instrument's highest register. Moreover, he had developed into a highly individual improviser who, when really inspired, had not only an abundance of creative ideas but more than enough technique to summon them instantly and unerringly from his clarinet. Primarily a lyric player, Shaw excelled in his peak years in the long, flowing, seamless soaring line."[63]

Long, flowing, soaring lines are obvious in his recording of "I Can't Get Started." Shaw sticks close to the melody in a tight arrangement that swings at a moderate tempo. Towards the end, a brief Ray Linn trumpet solo acknowledges Bunny, and with Shaw in the lead the band soars to the end. In this recording, Shaw seems to be following a lesson he learned by listening to the recordings of others: "The thing that each of these hit records had, it seemed to me, was a crystal-clear transparency. Not only in the recording, but in the arranging as well. You could hear every single last instrument on the record. The arrangement itself was simple, essentially; as a result even a lay listener could (so to speak) see all the way through the surface of the music right down to the bottom, as when you look into a clear pool of water and see the sand at the very bottom of the pool."[64] Because Shaw was with Bunny Berigan in 1936 when he recorded "I Can't Get Started," his version brings a kind of circular resolution to the life of the song during the Swing Era.

The same time big bands were reaching the end of their popularity, small groups were inventing a new way of playing jazz. The innovators of bebop, as the first phase of the new jazz was called, often favored a faster, more complex approach to improvisation. They used the higher intervals of the diatonic scale, such as flatted ninths and sharpened elevenths, to make their point. Unfortunately, the 1942-44 musicians strike prevented this new style of jazz from being recorded, and an important phase in the history of jazz was lost. Individuals such Thelonious Monk, Charlie Christian, Charlie Parker, and Dizzy Gillespie honed their skills in nightclubs and private parties witnessed by few people. What this limited audience heard, however, was not entirely new. Initially, the beboppers improvised within the thirty-two bar limit of most popular songs. And they sometimes based their compositions on the chord changes of popular songs. Charlie Parker's "Anthropology," for example, follows the chords of "I Got Rhythm."[65] Parker recorded "I Can't Get Started," but it is Gillespie's rendition that began a new chapter in the song's history.

Born in South Carolina on October 21, 1917, Gillespie took up the trumpet in his teens, becoming proficient enough by 1937 to be hired by Teddy Hill. He joined Cab Calloway in 1939 and then had stints with big bands led by Ella Fitzgerald, Claude Hopkins, Les Hite, Lucky Millinder, Charlie Barnet, Fletcher Henderson, and Benny Carter. After leading his own group for a short time in 1942, he joined Earl Hines and then Duke Ellington for a brief period. He co-led with Oscar Pettiford a combo and worked with other groups before joining Billy Eckstine's band in 1944.[66]

In deference to Bunny Berigan, Gillespie did not record "I Can't Get Started" until 1945. Like Bunny Berigan, he recorded two versions of the song in succeeding years and like him the first was in a small group, the second in a big band. In January 1945 he recorded four songs: his own "Salt Peanuts" and "BeBop," Tadd Dameron's "Good Bait," and "I Can't Get Started." The sextet included trombonist Trummy Young, tenor saxophonist Don Byas, pianist Clyde Haart, bassist Oscar Pettiford, and drummer Shelly Manne. Interestingly, the makeup of the group reflected the transition jazz was going through. Young was a swing player, Byas and Haart were suspended between the old and the new, and Manne, Pettiford and Gillespie were modernists. Well aware of the popularity of and skill involved in Bunny Berigan's rendition, Dizzy sought to demonstrate, according to Donald L. Maggin, "that the bebop language could express the tenderest emotions, that it was not limited to complex, up-tempo tunes; and he was inviting direct comparison to a classic swing record."[67] As explained by Dizzy, "I figured that a new idea on it wouldn't take anything away from Bunny Berigan but show there were possibilities for the tune."[68]

"Dizzy crafted a much subtler, more contemplative version of the song," noted Maggin, "sacrificing none of its beauty and creating his first masterpiece. Dameron's excellent arrangement has Byas and Young playing lovely counter melodies under Dizzy in both the A and B sections. In his solo, Dizzy modernized the A sections by using four pairs of chromatically linked descending chords in place of the original diatonic ones, and he achieved a subtle climax in the B section with a series of linked chromatic phrases. Authoritative without being melodramatic, Dizzy created, with his modern harmonies, a penetrating lyricism that plumbed even deeper levels of emotion than Berigan had reached."[69] But to suggest, as has Alyn Shipton, that after listening to Dizzy's rendition, Bunny's seems "harmonically shallow and intellectually stale," implies an inability to appreciate the historical and musical context from which each emerged.[70]

Comprehending the context in which pianist Lennie Tristano interpreted song, however, is more challenging. Born nearly blind in 1919 in Chicago to an Italian-American mother and an Italian immigrant father, Tristano lost his eyesight completely when he was about nine or ten years old. The loss of sight did not prevent him from developing his intellectual and musical skills in a school for the blind. Between 1934 and 1938, he studied not only the traditional subjects in history, math, and sciences, but he learned the rudiments of orchestration and to play the piano and cello. He also listened to the recordings of Louis Armstrong, Roy Eldridge, and Earl Hines. Between 1938 and the end of 1943, he studied at the American Conservatory of Music in Chicago. He graduated with a bachelor's degree in music performance in 1941 and continued on to graduate school for the next two years, but he quit school to play jazz, at least on a part-time basis. In the clubs and lounges around Chicago, he gained a reputation as a pianist of great talent with a promising future. His piano style, however, was not yet his own, having been greatly influenced by Art Tatum. By 1944 Tristano could play anything of Tatum's, but thereafter he began to perfect an individual style, a style that had come to fruition in 1946 when he moved to New York. There, he quickly became known to many jazz musicians as someone who was taking jazz in a new direction.[71]

In August 1946 he, with Billy Bauer on guitar and Leonard Gaskin on bass, cut a V-disk, one side containing "A Night in Tunisia," the other "I Can't Get Started." The melody is submerged in Tristano's chords, yet his solo is hypnotically melodic. The structure of the song, moreover, remains intact. He takes the song through its traditional dynamics and gets to the bridge on time. Because of the limited distribution of the recording, however, this version has received little attention and analysis. The second recording, however, is another matter. On October 8, 1946, with Bauer and Clyde Lombardi now on bass, the trio made fifteen recordings of four songs and a blues, but only two were selected. The third take of "Out on a Limb" and the second of "I Can't Get Started" were released the following year. Although the melody of "I Can't Get Started" is recognizable, Tristano's arrangement is so radical that it was even ahead of the rapid changes jazz was undergoing in the 1940s. Indeed, if any two records exemplify these changes they are Wilson's recording in 1941 and Tristano's in 1946. Interestingly,

118

Teddy Wilson in a blindfold listening test, often conducted by Leonard Feather on various musicians, was less than enthusiastic in what he heard: "They have everything but the kitchen sink in here—splashing weird chords around they seem to enjoy it. Use of all that harmony is indiscriminate, not significant. They must have had their ears glued to Delius and Ravel. . .sounded like really free improvisation, and they did run into some very good things at times."[72]

When jazz historian Barry Ulanov first heard the song and its companion piece, he "knew that the first notes in a bright new era of jazz had been struck. Here were the long lines side by side, the calculated but not contrived continuity, the improvised counterpoint crackling with suggestions of atonality, all strung together with a toe-snapping beat. Here was a full, fresh demonstration that jazz could parallel the development of classical music in the twentieth century without actually deriving from it."[73]

In a *Down Beat* article, Michael Levin explained that the song contains aspects of polyphony, polyrhythm, and advanced harmonies, and Tristano "uses constant intermixed figures with Bauer, and a melodic and harmonic line that depend on linear development rather than repeated riffs." Although there were times when the trio does not swing, "there is no reason to limit jazz to 2/4 and 4/4 for the rest of its existence." The record "represents the attempt of three musicians to take jazz as they have heard it, combine it with a developing classical tradition and still keep it freely improvisatory in nature."[74] A team of critics wrote in *Metronome* that they detected "linear construction and dissonance out of Hindemith."[75] Eunmi Shim has suggested that Tristano appreciated an aspect of the song beyond its chords and melody: "The use of such complicated harmonic structures without clear functional references is an important fact in understanding Tristano's daring use of harmonies. On the emotional, level, it effectively reflects on the sentiment of the lyrics, that is, unrequited love, by evoking a brooding mood."[76]

Gunther Schuller has placed the trio's recording of "I Can't Get Started" on a list of the "dozen or so major stations in the

development of jazz in the twenty years between 1926 an 1946."
By "stations" he meant "pieces, compositions, improvisations,
performances that in some crucial way moved jazz dramatically
forward." The list includes Armstrong's "West End Blues" for
rhythm, Duke Ellington's "Mood Indigo" for tone, color and
harmony, and Coleman Hawkins' "Body and Soul" for melodic
improvisation.[77]

"I Can't Get Started," Schuller wrote,

> is transformed into a completely new composition
> by Tristano's ministrations and manipulations of it.
> The original song is the merest pretext for a whole
> new concept of jazz in which tonality and atonality,
> harmony and counterpoint, meet on common
> ground, in brand new fusions. This is accomplished
> almost entirely by Tristano alone, his trio partners—
> Billy Bauer on guitar and Clyde Lombardi on
> bass—performing their traditional and limited
> roles: Bauer in single-line melodic statements,
> Lombardi in a simple, rather inertly plodding bass
> line, outlining the song's basic chordal scheme.
> On this unextraordinary foundation Tristano
> builds a remarkable improvised superstructure of
> great harmonic, melodic, and even to some extent
> rhythmic invention.[78]

Where to locate Tristano in the continuum of jazz has led to
little consensus. Ted Gioia noted:

> Most commentators and historians have
> listed him as a member of the 'cool' school that
> predominated during the 1950s. But this classification
> captures only a small part of Tristano's legacy. For
> the most part his music had little in common with
> the pared-down melody line, the warm lyricism,
> and relaxed tempos and chamber-music delicacy
> that characterized the 'cool' idiom. Schuller, for his
> part, evaluates Tristano as part of his study,

The Swing Era, and though a case could be made linking the pianist to swing period musicians such as Art Tatum and Mel Powell, this too remains an unsatisfying choice. Finally, one might see Tristano as a precursor of the later 'free' jazz movement. All of these supposed genealogies can point to some family likeness to justify their claims. However, to my ears, Tristano's closest allegiance was to none of the schools, but rather to the bebop movement; he shared its fascination with long melodic lines, its celebration of intensity, its refusal to compromise, and its imperative to experiment.[79]

At the same time jazz artists were experimenting with their song, Ira Gershwin and Vernon Duke continued to write for Broadway shows and Hollywood movies. Their lives would cross several times, but their careers sent them in different directions.

Chapter Seven
After the Follies: Careers in Flux

Once his duties in *Ziegfeld Follies of 1936* were finished, Ira Gershwin wrote a few songs with Phil Charig, Vicente Youmans, Harry Warren, and others, but was not sure he wanted to continue writing Broadway shows. He blamed the Great Depression for the sorry state of Broadway but also the Hollywood musical. He lamented the fleeing of songwriters and others to California. "Boy," he complained on one occasion "what the pix have done to the legit."[1] But he too fell victim to the siren song of Hollywood, as did his brother. Initially, however, Ira wondered how well he would work again with George, after collaborating with Vernon Duke and experiencing his rich harmonies. While working on "Let's Call the Whole Thing Off" for the Fred Astaire and Ginger Rogers' movie *Shall We Dance*, he initially thought that he was "being fed a sparser musical diet than with Duke," that the tune was thin and unimportant. But "gradually, notes began to fill out and rhythms sparkle."[2]

In 1936 Duke wrote some of the songs for *The Show is On*, which received a very positive review from Elinor Hughes of the *Boston Herald*. A ballet in the show, called "Tragedian," is credited to Vladimir Dukelsky.[3] And from the show came "Now," with a lyric by Ted Fetter. This beautiful and haunting love song remained popular during the 1930s but is now largely forgotten. The song repeats the same note when "now" is sung, emphasizing that now is the time to savor a love relationship that is bound to wane. Unfortunately, cut from the show was a jam session led by Bunny Berigan. Had it worked, the theater and jazz would have truly converged, at least for one act.

While the Gershwin brothers were living in Beverly Hills and working on *Damsel in Distress*, George came home from a party, sat down at the piano, and suggested to Ira that they get to work on a song. Ira recommended that they "do something about a fog. . .how about a foggy day in London or maybe a foggy day in London Town." George liked "London Town" better and soon had composed a melody. Ira wrote the lyric, and together they created a song in less than an hour. The next day the verse was completed.[4]

"A Foggy Day," as astutely assessed by Ted Gioia, is a variant on the city song which generally praises the metropolis. But Ira's lyric makes London seem as drab and dreary until the final bars: "For suddenly, I saw you there / And through foggy London Town / The sun was shining ev'rywhere." Beginning with "And through foggy London Town," the song turns into something resembling a military fanfare or the English folk tune "Country Gardens." The melody extends beyond the typical thirty-two bars.[5] And as Ira was wont to do, he gave the story an ending, in this case a surprise one.

As the quality of "A Foggy Day" clearly indicates, Hollywood did not always harm the creative efforts of the artists who relocated there from New York. Vernon Duke, however, regretted the exodus. When talents like Fred Astaire and the Gershwins left Broadway for Hollywood, the "remaining stars were left queasy. . . . The opulent reviews written around a Fanny Brice or a Beatrice Lillie were, too, dealt a mortal blow by Vincente Minnelli's removal to the West Coast."[6] But all was not right in Hollywood. Ira wrote to Vernon in October 1936, mentioning that many of his colleagues in Hollywood were struggling. At a recent party thrown by Gus Khan he had seen "every song writer I had ever met and met some I had never seen. Of course not all are doing well, but even those who haven't contracted refuse to go back and meantime get along on Society money." He noted that Khan's son played and sang "I Can't Get Started" and "Island in the West Indies" and wondered if Vernon had seen the movie *Swing Time*, music and lyrics by the Gershwins. The affection Ira held for Vernon is clearly reflected in the letter—he addressed him as "Ducky," and playfully called him the "Illegitimate Prince of the Georgias." Vernon was to give Fanny Brice a hug for him.[7]

Vernon's response was no less affectionate: "I still consider you the finest fellow alive and far too good for this wretched New York." He gently complained about Ira being "in Hollywood and liking it too much as far as this unhappy denizen of Manhattan is concerned." He liked *Swing Time* and noted "The Way You Look Tonight" and "A Fine Romance" (from the movie) were "selling big."[8]

Sometime in early 1937, Vernon wrote to Ira about the possibility of finding work in Hollywood. Ira's response was to the point: "its a bad place to take a gamble on unless they definitely want you. . . The fact that you are in New York is worth 25 to 50% more on your price when they get around to you. And if your next show is a hit there will be plenty of offers. And don't send songs on approval. Hold out." Ira mentioned that Jerome Kern was ill but on the road to recovery, and "All of us are well, Lee, George, Moss."[9]

But on July 11, 1937, George Gershwin at the age of 38 died from a brain tumor. A short time later, Merle Armitage asked numerous musicians and others to submit to him essays about George, which he compiled in a book dedicated to Ira. The contributors included Ira, Paul Whiteman, DuBose Heyward, Irving Berlin, Jerome Kern, Harold Arlen, but surprisingly not Vernon Duke. As Armitage noted, "Other friends and associates of George Gershwin were invited to contribute, who for reasons best known to themselves, failed to respond."[10] Duke may have referred to the book in his autobiography: "The terrible truth was that George was dead and posthumously eulogizing a career barely begun, seemed an ill-timed and premature postlude—for George was American youth itself, and his music was the voice of Young America, now inexplicably silenced."[11] After its publication, Ira told Vernon that "Armitage's book is all right. There's some good stuff in it but little of a critical nature. Since Armitage says he didn't set out to do a critical survey but more of a tribute to the man we can't cavil at the catholicity of the articles."[12]

Most of the articles focused on "Rhapsody in Blue" and *Porgy and Bess*, but several of the writers noted how Gershwin's songs defined America, that in some ways they could be considered historical documents. "It is not over-estimating his music to say that it expressed something distinctly new," wrote Ferde Grofé, "something typically of our land and people, and employed an unmistakable American idiom in melody, rhythm, and harmonization."[13] George Antheil suggested "For whatever his flaws, the flaws of George Gershwin are the flaws of America. He mirrored us, exactly. We need only to look into his music to see a whole period of our history exactly stated."[14] George was "our melodic spokesman," wrote Erma Taylor "and not only did he win the world's approval for musica americana, but more important to us, he justified us to ourselves. He bridged the chasm between jazz and the symphony, and brought the opera to the people. He made peace between the dance hall and the concert stage, the movie palace and the opera house. He democratized music, and he was the idol of that new democracy."[15] According to David Ewen, Gershwin "had his place—a far more important place than he himself felt—both as a musical influence and as an artistic creator. As an influence he has given shape and direction to American music, more so than an other American composer I can think of at the moment. He has evolved an American musical vocabulary which has become a part and parcel of America's self-expression. He literally discovered, alone and unaided, the artistic possibilities of jazz which he exploited fully. The Rhapsody in Blue, with the very first slide of the clarinet, emancipated jazz from the slums— and with such success that, before long, such respected masters of musical composition as Stravinsky, Ravel, Krenek and Kurt Weill were following his banner."[16]

The impact George Gershwin had on jazz is clearly demonstrated in the numerous jazz albums that feature only his songs. As Michael Feinstein has noted, "Perhaps because he was so thoroughly immersed in the jazz of his day, Gershwin's songs lend themselves to jazz interpretations better than the works of many other songwriters of the era. Whatever the reason, the literature of jazz attests to Gershwin's adaptability by the sheer volume of his compositions that have been played and recorded by the greatest jazz musicians—whether Art Tatum improvising endlessly on 'Liza,' Lester Young and Teddy Wilson duetting on 'Love Is Here to Stay,' Charlie Parker soaring through 'Embraceable You,' or countless versions of 'I Got Rhythm' and other standards based on the song's harmonic structure (or chord changes.)"[17] Gershwin did not live long enough to see the influence his music had on jazz, but it would have been enormous if only "I Got Rhythm" had emerged from his fertile mind. Will Friedwald has suggested that Gershwin might "be seen as a transitional figure between older colleagues Berlin and Kern (not to mention the old-at-heart Richard Rodgers), who wanted their music played exactly as written, and slightly younger ones, like Hoagy Carmichael, Johnny Mercer, and Harold Arlen, who were in and of the jazz world."[18] To the latter group, Vernon Duke should be added.

In 1937 he and Ira teamed up again—this time to complete the music George was preparing for *The Goldwyn Follies*, an early Technicolor film. Lee Shubert and Billie Burke, Ziegfeld's widow, had sold the motion picture, radio, and television rights to the title "Ziegfeld Follies" to Metro-Goldwyn Mayer. As reported by in the *New York Times*, out of the voluminous George Gershwin files, "Duke salvaged the tune for another 'Follies' song, 'Love Walked In' which he arranged and harmonized; two other songs, 'I Was Doing all Right,' and 'Love Is Here to Stay,' had refrains but no verses; Duke supplied these, and Ira Gershwin, of course, did all the lyrics. The music for two ballets, 'Romeo and Juliet,' (in jazz) and 'Water Nymph,' were especially composed by Duke to fit the steps executed by Ballanchine [sic] and are (historical note) the first ballets expressively created for the screen."[19]

Ira, however, was disappointed in the lyric he wrote for "Love Walked In." Because the song was placed in a spot with no plot or characterization to latch on to, he knew the "tune would be a tough one to set," he recalled many years later. "After a long struggle (two weeks, three weeks?) I came up with the present lyric and was certainly not too proud of it. . . .Here, finding myself endowing love with an ambulatory ability was more than a bit much." Lines such as "Love walked right in and drove the shadows a way / Love walked right in and brought my sun-ni-est day," exemplify Ira's concerns. But a year or so after the song was presented, it made the *Hit Parade* where it remained for over twenty weeks.[20]

Concerned about the decline in Ira's productivity as a Broadway lyricist after the death of his brother, in late 1938 Vernon Duke told him that he was "too much of an admirer of your lyrical and other gifts not to get worried about your inactivity." He concluded his letter by emphasizing "that my one dream is to do another show with you; my other dream is to do another show with you. Am I on the black list or can I go on living in hope? Balanchine and I both pray for your return and for a grand reunion."[21] In early 1940 Vernon pleaded with Ira to join with him and Balanchine in the production of a musical about African Americans to be called "Little Joe." He bragged that the libretto is "utterly fascinating and, with my customary modesty, I will admit that I have written a stupendous score." To write the lyrics, the producers considered Johnny Mercer or Yip Harburg but encouraged Vernon to see if Ira might be interested.[22] Duke was unsuccessful in recruiting Ira, but he persuaded Ethel Waters to join the cast. After her success in *Mamba's Daughters* of the preceding season, she wanted to remain in dramatic roles. But after several hours of Duke's insistence, which must have been infused with considerable charm, she agreed.[23]

With its name changed to *Cabin in the Sky* and starring Waters, it was about to open on Broadway when cast and crew concluded that something was missing. Waters needed a song to uplift the spirits of the character she was playing. Duke dug up an old song he had written with Ted Fetter called "Fooling Around with Love." Waters suggested it be called "Taking a Chance on Love," and John Latouche reworked the lyric. According to historian Ethan Mordden, "the insertion of this one number utterly rebalanced the show, married its contemporaneity with its timelessness, its spirituality with its earthiness."[24]

Although "Taking a Chance on Love" would become as popular as Duke's other standards, it was dismissed by Alec Wilder. He admitted that Waters helped the song, but considered it "a contrivance, practically a potboiler. At no point is there any aspect of Duke's invention and musicality."[25] Granted, the melody is locked firmly in the AABA, thirty-two bar format, and the harmonies of the bridge rely on the well used II, V, I chord pattern. But more than most of Duke's songs, this one, because of its melody and chords, allows artists to swing it upbeat, as did the Benny Goodman orchestra in its 1940 recording. A fine vocal by Hellen Ward, one of the best big-band vocalists, and featuring Cootie Williams on trumpet and of course Benny on clarinet, the recording became a hit.

The lyric fits the melody perfectly, and as with many songs of the period, its verse is important. With phrases such as "Thought the Game was Over,' "Lady Luck Gone Away," "Cards on the Table," and "Dealing a New Hand," it informs the listener that love is a gamble. The chorus, especially, the bridge, also contains gambling allusions: "Now I thought the cards were a frame-up / And I never would try / But now I'm taking the game up / And the ace of hearts is high."

As recalled by Duke: "After the opening, having kissed every member of the cast, cried with Ethel and slapped Max Meth, the frenzied conductor, on the back a dozen of times, Balanchine, Zorina and I repaired to '21' and sat in a happy haze, drinking Pommery Greno of the right year to be joined at 2:30 A.M. by Vinton, his eyes shining, who waved the ecstatic Brooks Atkinson's review and he read it to us in a quivering, happy voice."[26]

"Perhaps 'Cabin in the Sky' could be a better than it is," enthused Atkinson, "but this correspondent cannot imagine how. For the musical fantasy. . .is in an original and joyous in an imaginative vein that suits the theatre's special genius. Lynn Root began it by writing an extraordinarily fresh book. . . .For it would be difficult to prove that the book is happier in style than George Balanchine's lyrical direction or the excellent performance by a singularly well-chose Negro cast." Atkinson had "never heard a song better sung than 'Taking a Chance on Love.'" Ethel Waters "stood that song on its head last evening and ought to receive a Congressional medal by way of reward."[27]

The play ran for only 156 performances, but three years later Vincente Minnelli, brilliantly transferred *Cabin in the Sky* to the screen. Ethel Waters reprised her role and sang "Taking a Chance on Love" but without the verse. By this time the song had been well tested, 150,000 copies having been sold by January 1944. Still, according to a critic for *New York Times*, the song "has worn well in three years, but "it was sung so refreshingly and with such plaintive feeling by Miss Waters that it sounds like a brand new number."[28] Unfortunately, Louis Armstrong had only a small speaking part in the movie, but as "Georgia Brown" Lena Horne got one of her better roles.

Ira missed out on *Cabin in the Sky*, but in 1941 he returned to Broadway and joined Kurt Weill for *Lady in the Dark*, which included Danny Kaye performing a song few in the world could pull off. It is called "Tschaikowsky," and in it he rattled off forty-nine composers in thirty-nine seconds. Two lines went like this: "There's Medtner, Balakireff, Zolotareff and Kvoschinsky. And Sokoloff and Kopyloff, Dukelsky and Klenowsky."[29]

What Ira thought of *Lady Be Good*, the movie released that year that had nothing to do with his and George's musical of 1924, is not known, which probably is just as well. Although "Lady Be Good and "Fascinating Rhythm" are featured, songs of other composers were also included, including "The Last Time I Saw Paris," by Jerome Kern and Oscar Hamerstein II, which won the Academy Award for the best song that year. A typical Hollywood version of the Broadway musical theater, the film's best sequence is the dancing of Eleanor Powell to "Fascinating Rhythm," with a boogie-woogie beat. Thus, jazz and the musical theater temporarily merged, at least through a Hollywood lens. A better adaption to the screen was *Girl Crazy*, released in 1943 and starring Mickey Rooney and Judy Garland and with most of the score by George Gershwin.

Production of the movie *Cover Girl*, starring Gene Kelly and Rita Hayworth, began in 1943. Ira joined Jerome Kern for the music and "Long Ago (And Far Away)" became a hit, especially with servicemen overseas. The haunting melody has been called a Kern masterpiece, but Ira was initially not pleased with his efforts. After writing five or six lyrics, he felt "it was just a collection of words adding up to very little." But later he realized that he had followed the advice of the producer and "had come through, as requested, with a good, simple lyric."[30]

In 1945 Ira provided the lyrics for Kurt Weill's *The Firebrand of Florence*, and the following year he and Arthur Schwartz composed the music for *Park Avenue.* Neither show did very well. "After the failure of 'Park Avenue,'" he told Vernon, "I returned to Calif. and here I have been ever since. Since Nov. '46 I haven't so much as looked at a lyric but have been taking it easy. There have been several propositions for shows but after the 'Firebrand' and 'Park Avenue' I feel I can't afford a B' way show unless it's the last word in the way of a new idea or something." In passing he mentioned "The other night some people came over and Kay Swift played and I sang the songs from 'Z. Follies' of '36. 'I Can't Get Started,' 'Isle West Indies', 'Gazooka,' 'Words Without Music,' 'Moment of Moments'—all sounded fresh and undated."[31]

Although *Park Avenue* was Ira's last Broadway show, Hollywood provided him with an outlet for his talents. In 1947 he contributed several of George's unpublished songs to the Betty Grable film *The Shocking Miss Pilgrim.* He wrote the lyrics to "Aren't You Kind of Glad We Did?," "For You, For Me, For Evermore," "Changing My Tune," and "Back Bay Polka."

Also showing that year was *The Ziegfeld Follies of 1946*, and as fate would have it Vincente Minnelli was the film's director. Like the stage production, there is no plot, only songs, sketches, a ballet, beautiful ladies, and dancing. So massive was the production that each segment of the movie had an individual director, with Minnelli in overall control. Because it had been only ten years since Minnelli had been associated with the stage production, perhaps *The Ziegfeld Follies of 1946* reflects to some degree the stage revue. In particular, the Fanny Brice sketch about losing a winning ticket to the Irish Sweepstakes came directly from the 1936 *Follies.* Red Skelton and Keenan Wynn also had comedy sketches. And to introduce the show, William Powell, who starred in *The Great Ziegfeld* in 1936, was again cast as Ziegfeld, except now he is in heaven reminiscing about his productions. Fred Astaire dances with Lucille Bremer and with Gene Kelly; Lena Horne sings "Love" in a Caribbean setting; and in a sketch called "The Great Lady Has an Interview," Judy Garland is surrounded by male dancers and exhibits the confidence of a young woman already a star.

Because Technicolor was still in its infancy, the *San Diego Union* mentioned that it "added greatly to the spectacular side of the staging." Moreover, the costumes were "glamorous and the chorus is a busy group of fine looking girls. For two hours of good music, fine dancing and refreshing comedy 'Ziegfeld's Follies of 1946' is grand entertainment."[32] From a modern perspective the movie seems dated, but it is still worth watching, if for nothing more than the dancing of Gene Kelly and Fred Astaire. The dance is highly athletic, as was Kelly's style, with the much older Astaire demonstrating that he was far from through.

Fred Astaire and Ginger Rogers starred in *The Barkleys of Broadway,* released in 1949 and featuring the music of composer Harry Warren. Ira provided the lyrics to the new songs, but on one song he had little to do. He and George had written "They Can't Take That Away From Me" for the 1937 movie *Shall We Dance*. It was interpolated into the movie, to the chagrin of Harry Warren, and was nominated for an Academy Award for that year.

In 1941 and 1942, Duke wrote songs for *Banjo Eyes,* starring Eddie Cantor, and a disaster called *The Lady Comes Across* with comic Joe E. Lewis. Following America's entrance in World War II, Duke, who had become an American citizen in 1939, was drafted into the Coast Guard as a seaman. After eighteen months of service he was released with a medical discharge, but was coaxed back into the service with a commission as a lieutenant and a promise of considerable free time to pursue his musical career. In 1943, he joined Howard Dietz in producing songs for *Dancing in the Streets*, with Mary Martin, but the show closed out of town. *Jackpot*, opened in 1944 and was fairly successful. That year he also wrote the score for a service musical called *Tars and Spars*, which included the then unknown but future television star Sid Caesar. As reported in the *Boston Herald*, audiences in Philadelphia, Pittsburgh, and New York loved it, and it went on a national tour. All fifty-five members of the cast were Coast Guard personnel, including twenty-four "of the nation's cutest ladies," personally selected by Vernon.[33] Duke unabashedly admitted that during the selection process he had enjoyed observing "a few dozen of the prospects' legs, now that their owners, having shed their Molyneux-designed uniforms, looked like any other female beach-combers. Selecting the chorus was a tough job, as some of the prettier candidates were allergic to stage appearances, some of the hopelessly unattractive ones, were, on the contrary, dying to get into the show." Regarding the songs, Duke insisted that he and Howard Dietz wrote "some good things for Tars and Spars—'Arm in Arm,' 'You Gotta Have a Reason to Be a Civilian' and 'Palm Beach' among them." But he was greatly disappointed in the movie of the same name: "There was no connection whatever between our fresh and uninhabited little revue and [producer] Bren's flat-footed essay in musical flagwaving."[34]

Sadie Thompson opened in New York in late 1944 and was a moderate financial success. Based on a play taken from W. Somerset Maugham's story "Rain," it is set on an island in the South Seas in which a missionary seeks to reform a prostitute with tragic results. Although the grim story is hardly the stuff of a musical, a critic noted that all concerned in this production, including Vernon Duke who composed the score, "met all the difficulties involved with signal success. '*Sadie Thompson*' is a very stirring contribution to the current theater."[35] From the show came "The Love I Long For," with the lyric by Howard Dietz. *Sweet Bye and Bye* never got to Broadway, closing in Philadelphia in 1946. Duke and Ogden Nash created several great songs, including "Low and Lazy" and "Round About." But the music clashed with the futuristic libretto by S. J. Perelman and caricaturist Al Hirschfeld. The director and producer had never directed or produced before. The male lead had no stage experience except as a mime, and the leading lady had a nervous breakdown and may have attempted suicide. She ended up in a sanatorium. The score, songs and libretto ended up in storage in New Jersey.

After the war, Duke returned to composing classical works, including violin and cello concertos, a ballet, a harpischord sonata, and "Ode to the Milky Way," conducted by Leonard Bernstein at the City Center in New York in 1946. That year also saw the premiere of his Third Symphony.

Between 1947 and 1949, he journeyed to Europe three times, mainly to Paris. When he permanently returned to the United States, Duke settled in Los Angeles where he met new friends and linked-up with old ones. To attend the parties of Vincente Minnelli, John Houseman, and especially to those hosted by Ira and Lee Gershwin, he learned to drive. Ira preferred small parties of five or six people, recalled Vernon, who were "known for their love of argument, and letting them loose in his drawing room; the feathers fly while Ira grunts contentedly, puffing on an aromatic Montecristo." On one occasion, Duke got into an argument with pianist, composer, arranger, actor, author, and self-deprecating neurotic Oscar Levant. As they screamed at each other at the top of their lungs, a worried Leonore was about to send for help, but "Ira beamed delightedly, took the Montecristo out of his mouth, and said with a purr: 'Now, isn't that better than a stupid big party, where nobody knows anybody?'"[36]

The year 1952 was a busy one for Vernon Duke. He and Sammy Cahn composed original songs for the movie *April in Paris,* starring Doris Day, which included the famous song of the same name he wrote with E.Y. Harburg. He and Cahn also provided six songs for *She's Working Her Way Through College,* with Virginia Mayo and Ronald Reagan. And he was called back to Broadway to compose songs for *Two's Company,* starring Bette Davis. A strange choice for a musical play, Davis "did the best she could in an unfamiliar idiom," recalled Duke, "and that her best was often very good indeed."[37] Duke told a reporter that "a certain producer wanted her for a picture and when she went to the stage, he was determined to kill the show at any cost." That scheme failed, but Hollywood buzzed that Davis was temperamental and wanted out because she had a big cash offer to do a picture. Although the "show was constantly on the brink of disaster," Duke admitted, it was because the sketches kept changing and because Davis came down with a terrible case of laryngitis. Davis never fought with anybody, but she would not do a sketch that made fun of Hollywood.[38]

Despite mixed reviews, it ran for three months to capacity attendance. Much of the credit for the show's limited success should go to the composer, noted historian Ethan Mordden: "if anyone could figure out what 'Bette Davis music' must sound like, it was Duke. Too often, when writing for a non-singer, a composer invests in ditties with a three note range. . . .It's star insurance, but it isn't music. Davis and Duke might have chosen that option, but on the contrary, he gave her real music that she could really navigate, and Davis, refusing to ham-and-egg her way through the challenge of carrying a big musical, threw herself into the doings." Even though "the New York smarty-pants opinion was that Davis was hopelessly out of her league as a musical comedy star," her sketches "focused on her possibilities rather than on her limitations." For ninety-one performances, she carried the show, but when she became ill it was closed. Because the audience came to see Davis, no replacement was deemed possible.[39]

Not content to write only Broadway shows, Vernon also entered the recording field, releasing in 1953 an album called *Vernon Duke Plays Vernon Duke*, which included "I Can't Get Started" in a medley of four songs. He recorded the songs on a strangely designed piano which had an extra keyboard. By pressing a special pedal, every note was augmented by a corresponding note an octave higher, but the sound is tinny. Given Duke's classical training, this choice of instruments seems odd, and the result is disappointing. And instead of including "Words Without Music" and "That Moments of Moments," the only other song from the 1936 *Follies* is "Island in the West Indies," not my favorite Duke composition. He did include two of his most famous songs, "Autumn in New York" and "April in Paris," but they too suffer from this strange sounding piano. A much better compilation came the following year when jazz pianist Dick Hyman recorded fourteen of his songs, including a sensitive rendition of "I Can't Get Started."

The same cannot be said of cabaret singer Bobby Short's 1955 version. He interprets it in a playful, whimsical way—affecting an English accent in places and giving it a blues ending. Moreover, his ponderous piano solo clashes with his lighthearted vocalization. In the liner notes, Duke wrote: "Since Bobby paid me the flattering honor of recording seven of my songs out of the total of thirteen of which this album is composed my enthusiasm for him may be interpreted as somewhat colored by his excessive partisanship of my Muse." Because Vernon acknowledged that Short played the songs "as though he wrote—or rewrote—them himself," he may not have been pleased with every rendition. But he may have liked "Autumn in New York," which Short sang with great sensitivity. Other than "I Can't Get Started," the only other song from the *Follies of 1936* is "Island in the West Indies," which Vernon noted has a "virtuoso lyric" by Ira Gershwin.[40] This song is far better arranged and sung than the much more famous one.

Somehow during his busy life as recorder and composer, Duke found the time to write his autobiography, *Passport to Paris,* published in 1955. Much of it deals with his extraordinary life in the two worlds of classical and theater music: "ACCORDING to Who's Who, I have spent my 'entire career' (come come, I'm still spending it) writing two kinds of music: the serious or unrewarding kind as Vladimir Dukelsky and the unserious but lucrative variety as Vernon Duke. Almost every interview I've ever had has brought forth some tired reference to 'the Jekyll and Hyde of Music,' 'the Two-Headed Janus of Music,' etc." But, as he pointed out, "There have been quite a few cases of composers who successfully managed to write in both the high-and low-brow genre, but I am entirely unique in one respect. Gershwin always remained Gershwin whether he wrote *Porgy* or 'I Got Rhythm'; Weill was easily recognizable as Weill whether he tackled *Mahagonny* or *One Touch of Venus*, and even Lennie Bernstein is his ingratiating self whether he tears into *Jeremiah* or *On the Town*; but Dukelsky in no way resembles Duke."[41]

Duke claimed that his versatility, "far from a boon, has in reality been infuriating to most musical people. Just why that is I have no way of knowing, but the critical boys seem to think there is something monstrous and unnatural about a composer writing two different kinds of music under two different names. It annoys them not to be able to say that I go slumming when writing jazz, and it annoys them still more not to be able to classify me as an ambitious peasant, gazing at the musical Olympus behind a Lindy's herring."[42]

Duke ends his autobiography with a confession that he was an unabashed name dropper. He also announced that "I'm dropping the name of Vladimir Dukelsky and henceforth will sign all music that may still flow from my pen—regardless of its nature—as Vernon Duke."[43] In reviewing the book, Francis Steegmuller detected duality in Vernon's life: "In the pages given to the earlier years, before the personality became so openly hyphenated, when the ecstatic young composer is still simply creating—not creating on this level or that—the book partakes of all the youthful élan of its hero; but it is a tribute to the second personality, second in the sense of being openly two, that that spectacle of such fresh youth is given the vividness of such perspective."[44]

When Ira received an inscribed copy of the book from Vernon, he wrote to his friend: "When you read us the two chapters last year I told many that I was sure the ultimate result would be a book of great interest, and now that I've read it I haven't been let down. It should get grand notices and I hope it becomes an enormous seller."[45] Dropped from the autobiography were two-hundred racy pages of Duke's numerous romantic involvements. To his question why the censorship, the editors replied: "We've been in Boston over 100 years and we expect to stay here."[46] On October 30, 1957, at age fifty-four, Duke finally gave up his bachelor days—and ways—and married a twenty-three year old soprano, Kay McCracken.

That year he wrote incidental music and two songs for *Time Remembered,* by French playwright Jean Anouih and starring Helen Hayes, Richard Burton, and Susan Strasberg. It ran for 247 performances and was well received by the critics. One of the songs, "Ages Ago," is another, little-known gem by Duke who also wrote the melancholy lyric. I suspect he had learned from Ira Gershwin some of the art of lyric writing, because the song has a surprise ending: "I pace the street and hope to meet someone I could completely and madly adore / But I can't change / there's no danger because I know / I love the girl [boy] I loved ages ago."[47]

In 1958, classical composer, conductor, and jazz pianist André Previn recorded ten of Duke's songs, including "Ages Ago" and "Round About." Although Duke was pleased with the outcome,   he mentioned in his liner notes that Previn's initial cut of "April in Paris" was "too faithful to the original, too 'ballady, perhaps" and suggested he record it again but with the verse, which he thought had "even more of the Parisian *ambiance* then the rest of the piece." The new interpretation concludes the album and is, according to Duke, the best instrumental version of his song. But "Other typically Previan transformations include *I Like the Likes of You* which is here imbued with a totally unexpected Sunday-go-to-meetin' flavor; [and] the highly personal and non-Beriganesque conception of *I Can't Get Started*," although what he meant by "non-Beriganesque" escapes me.[48] In a slow tempo, Previn creates a dark, moody atmosphere.

The following year, Vernon congratulated Ira on the publication of *Lyrics on Several Occasions*: "Your book is really quite wonderful and I read the entire volume, lyrics included, in three hours. The reference to me were (mostly) flattering and certainly illuminating. I could have done without that bit concerning my 1928 views of Tansman. . . .only because I was then absurdly young, also cocky and unafraid."[49] While Vernon was working on *Passport to Paris*, Ira had sent him a section of his diary, but he stipulated that incorporation must include both paragraphs. In the second one Duke is critical of the Polish-French composer Alexandre Tansman. Because Vernon failed to include the paragraph, Ira, apparently in a playful mood, felt "free now to offer the world this hitherto undisclosed critical disclosure."[50]

At the time, Vernon's mood was probably far from playful, because his Broadway career was not going very well. His off-Broadway show of 1956, *The Littlest Revue,* had managed only thirty-two performances. Of the nine songs Duke wrote for the show, only one stood out—"Born Too Late." But he always found other outlets for his intellectual energies. And who better than Duke to write the liner notes for the 1959 jazz version for Georges Bizet's opera, *Carmen*? "I think the first real jazz version of Carmen by Barney Kessel is a knockout, all right, but no one gets hurt," he noted. "I for one, am enchanted with it. Is it 'respectful' as regards Bizet? Well... let's say it's full of love, rather than respect. Certainly, Barney's guitar 'epigraphs' are as close to the original as possible, with only a slight harmonic deviation now and again. The airs, once intoned, are then in for a joyous and uninhibited airing, true jazz-fashion. The human voice is not missed. . . .Previn's resourceful piano and Manne's melodic drums, sing away exuberantly, unhampered by a recitative's shackles. And, by great good fortune, we are here spared verbal modernization of disputable authenticity and get authentically inspired swinging instead."[51]

When not writing liner notes in English, Duke wrote verse in Russian. The two volumes published in Munich elicited in 1962 a response from the poet Vladimir Markov: "The musician who in his field has tried just about everything intrudes into literature. Composers who toyed with poetry were no rarity in Russia. . . .But when the composer appears with a printed collection of his verses, especially when he is not such a novice [in literature] it is a unique situation. Even more unique is the fact that his poetry is original, written with technical brilliance, happily festive, and goes against a mainstream of Russian poetic diaspora."[52]

When not writing poems in Russian, Duke found the time to write the music for *Zenda,* an operetta based on *The Prisoner of Zenda* by Anthony Hope that was published in 1894. Starring Alfred Drake and Chia Rivera, its pre-Broadway tryout opened in early August 1963. After playing in Los Angeles and Pasadena, it closed after three months, suffering from a confusing plot, staging problems, and bickering between the director and librettist. None of Duke's songs has lasted, although Ethan Mordden considered "Let Her Not Be Beautiful" "a fine ballad of worry and need and almost on the Kern level."[53]

This was Duke's last musical, but it was far from his last intellectual effort. That year he published *Listen Here: A Critical Essay on Music Depreciation*. Included are chapters on classical composers, conductors, and their critics, and on opera, the ballet, and the American musical. For example, he took on French and British intellectuals, critical of just about everything American, including the musical theater. Though the French elite were concerned about being Americanized, Duke pointed out that in France the "entertainment-hungry masses do patronize the American 'action' picture over the homemade variety two to one." And "there exists a healthy respect for yet another U.S.A.-perfected semi-cultural product—Musical Comedy. From *No, No, Nanette* through *Show Boat, Oklahoma!* and *Guys and Dolls* to *My Fair Lady* and *West Side Story*, America climbs to the top with no indications of impending change." Because the French had virtually invented the musical theater, Vernon acknowledged they could "hardly be blamed for frowning on the present-day usurpation of it by the Americans." The only rival the French had were the Viennese who proved that the waltz could be sung as well as danced. Although "the Russians reigned at the ballet, the French in Cochran's revues," with the musical comedy "America was in the driver's seat."[54]

He was troubled, however, by the direction the American musical was then taking. Beginning in the 1960s, the writers of popular songs increasingly found themselves replaced by younger composers, such as Stephen Sondheim, who integrated their songs so thoroughly into the librettos that hits seldom emerged from their shows. While the librettos, sets, and dancing of the modern shows were often of high caliber, the music was "gradually being relegated to the role of a necessary but unimportant ornament. For we are entering the Era of the Musicless Musical."[55]

His other musical love, however, was flourishing: "That jazz is the strongest new musical influence the world over is undeniable—and jazz is American, although it may not be music to some." He admitted that there is no all-embracing definition of jazz, but "What jazz is, what was its function in musical America's coming of age, and to what extent must it be reckoned with as an organic stimulus in contemporary music in general, is of such importance that no writer can avoid speculating and pragmatizing on it."[56]

Duke's appreciation of jazz must have contributed significantly to his understanding how his songs were being interpreted. Not only was he unconcerned that they were modified, in some cases he welcomed the changes introduced to them: "It has always been my firm belief that the piano copy of a standard—or a showtune—is merely the germ, the skeleton of what the composer intended; piano copies have to be playable and simple in the extreme to be within the reach of the buying public. Thus, I regard every recorded version of a song as legitimate variations on a theme—a time honored musical form, as any purists will concede. In contrast with some of my colleagues, I especially appreciate those recordings of my light music that bring out unsuspected riches in my original, thanks to the performer's inspired meddling with it. I consider such meddling a compliment, not an imposition."[57]

That flexibility was demonstrated in 1966 when Duke was featured in a blindfold test conducted by Leonard Feather for *Down Beat*. With no prior knowledge of the records, he was asked to listen to some of his best-known popular songs. He commented on the recordings of "April in Paris," "Autumn in New York," "What is There to Say," "Taking a Chance on Love," "Cabin in the Sky," "Island in the West Indies," and "I Can't Get Started." Duke heard two recent renditions of the latter, one by Al Hirt (from *Honey in a Horn*), the other a medley by Dizzy Gillespie that included "Round Midnight" (from *Something Old, Something New*). He did not recognize Hirt, guessing that it might be Maynard Ferguson, but considered it one of the best versions he had heard. He liked the "oddly metallic trumpet sound throughout—no shading, no variations. It was particularly effective when the vocal background came in, sounding almost as if they had put mutes on the voices. It was most imaginative."[58] A reviewer of Hirt's rendition claimed that it was "just about as artistically close as anyone ever will get to the matchless Bunny Berigan play."[59] I could not disagree more. Hirt's version seems designed more to demonstrate his considerable technical skills than to give the song any meaning. In no way is it close to Berigan's version.

Regarding the "I Can't Get Started"/"Round Midnight" medley, Duke was his usually perceptive self:

> Now this is certainly the greatest of them all! If I gave one of the other recordings five stars. I would have to give this one 5 1/2—if such a thing is possible.

> This is a musician's joy. It is extraordinary—it has no end of imagination, and it is completely unpredictable. The way the saxophonist went into 3/4 there. Amazing!

> The whole performance has a fresh, invigorating quality. From the composer's standpoint this is certainly one of the most imaginative things I have heard.

> It sounds like Dizzy Gillespie, but the performance has a sort of fey charm and is much more elegant than what I normally associate with the earlier Dizzy.

> Dizzy always used to call me 'Mr. 603.' That was back in the bop era, and 603 was the number of *I Can't Get Started* in his books.[60]

That "I Can't Get Started" had become a jazz favorite obviously pleased Duke. But the legacies of its creators would rest not on any one song but on the many—well known and obscure—that artists would perform and record over the years.

Chapter Eight
Legacies: The Tunesmith, the Lyricist and Their Songs

Because of their distinctive temperaments, personalities, and musical orientations, Vernon Duke and Ira Gershwin reacted differently to the liberties vocalists and instrumentalists took with songs they wrote independently and collectively. Whereas Vernon was not adverse to artists experimenting with his melodies and harmonies and probably did not care much what happened to the lyrics, Ira became upset and irritable when vocalists altered his lyrics and instrumentalists changed the tempos and moods of his songs. For example, in 1947 he complained to Vernon that "Arrangers and bands have for the past 15 years, taken far too many liberties with melody and harmony. Not all of course, but too many. But there does seem to be an improvement the past few years. The song and the singer are coming in to their own again, as evidence by the popularity of the albums wherein the original cast and orchestrations of musical shows are used—no liberties taken—just the music and lyrics as done on the stage and in the pit."[1]

Ira, however, was not averse to changing his lyric to "I Can't Get Started" to fit changing circumstances. In 1948, he fashioned a female version for Judy Gershwin, wife of his brother Arthur, who in September was appearing in New York's "Ruban Bleu." Before marrying into the famous family, she had carved out a musical career for herself, singing for two years with the Xavier Cugat orchestra as Judy Lane. She told George Simon of *Metronome* that she had "always compared other lyrics with Ira's," that she liked "to sing real personal ballads, not things like Stardust." Judy possessed "an intelligent approach to singing which few of her rivals, current or potential, even bother about," noted Simon. "She makes good sense out of lyrics. Instead of phrasing just with the melody, she

Judy Gershwin, <u>Metronome</u>, September, 1945

studies a song, finds out what the lyricist means to say, and then phrases accordingly." Although the new lyric made sense,it was hardly Ira's best effort: "The men rush up from near and far/When I sell kisses at a bazaar/For me they strike the band up/I'm just a stand-up with you/ My legs have Dietrich out on a limb/My lips are soft, my figure is trim/But you've got me down-hearted/'Cause I can't get started with you." By admitting to Judy "This is the toughest assignment I've had," Ira, the perfectionist, may have implied dissatisfaction with his effort.[2]

If Ira heard Sarah Vaughan's 1947 version of "I Can't Get Started," he certainly would have been dissatisfied, given the way she alters the melody and the way Ted Dale's arrangement clashes sharply with her singing style. Ironically, in the album, *The Divine Sarah*, Vaughan ventured from pure jazz to a more commercially oriented style. But according to Gunther Schuller, her art was "too subtle, too sophisticated to make it in the big—really—big mass pop market. God knows, Sarah—or her managers—have tried to break into that field. But she never can make it or will make it. . .because she's too good."[3]

Even her jazz vocalizations did not always please her contemporaries. Mel Tormé loves Vaughan, but as a product of the bebop period "her singing was occasionally incomprehensible to the average listener."[4] It is not surprising, therefore, that Ira did not care for her recordings of his brother's music because, noted Michael Feinstein, "she did vocal tricks with the notes." On one occasion, he had to remove from the turntable one of her albums, because "Ira was so dismayed by hearing those interpretations."[5] Still, one wonders what she might have done with "Words without Music."

When Feinstein played a Sinatra rendition of "A Foggy Day," Ira said 'It was not as good as Fred Astaire, but it was louder.'"[6] Whether he was referring to the movie version or a later recording was not noted, but if it was Astaire's 1952 rendition, then on occasion Ira could be responsive to jazz. The album—*The Astaire Story*—was presented as a collection of songs introduced by Astaire in his stage shows and movies, including five by the Gershwin brothers—"Let's Call the Whole Thing Off," "'S Wonderful," "They All Laughed," "Nice Work if You Can Get It," and "A Foggy Day." But the album is not Astaire's alone. He shares it with great jazz musicians Oscar Peterson, Charlie Shavers, Flip Phillips, Barney Kessel, Ray Brown, and Alvin Stoller. Obviously remembered as a great dancer, Astaire is also a perfect example of how sensitive rhythmic phrasing can compensate for an average voice and a limited range. As in the days before the vocalist became the star and would sing through much of a recording, in all the songs Astaire gives the musicians ample time to develop their solos. This is a fine jazz album.

In 1952, Ira improved his female version of "I Can't Get Started." It and other songs of his are featured in an album called *Lyrics by Ira Gershwin*. Several performers sing ten songs, three composed by George Gershwin, two by Jerome Kern, two by Kurt Weill, one each by Aaron Copland, Arthur Schwartz, and Vernon Duke. Most of the songs are relatively obscure, except "Long Ago and Far Away" and "I Can't Get Started," sung by Broadway star Nancy Walker. The new verse ends with "Super Gal/Is Paunchy and Losing Morale." The second chorus includes: "When I sell kisses at a bazaar/The wolves line up from nearby and far/Their methods I have charted/But I can't get started with you."

lyrics by IRA GERSHWIN

NANCY WALKER
and
LOUISE CARLYLE
DAVID CRAIG
musical arrangements by
DAVID BAKER
produced by
LEON SEIDEL

Music by   AARON COPLAND   JEROME KERN
VERNON DUKE   ARTHUR SCHWARTZ
GEORGE GERSHWIN   KURT WEILL   WALDEN RECORDS

Although Walker's rendition is rather uninspiring, and she extends the song too long with the inclusion of the third chorus, hers is more satisfying than those of some jazz artists. The best part of Anita O'Day's 1955 version of "I Can't Get Started" is the verse, but with the chorus comes rather saccharine strings that do little to support her interpretation. Ella Fitzgerald's recording suffers from a surprisingly heavy-handed arrangement by Nelson Riddle. Often inclined to overstatement, she seems more interested in mouthing the words than interpreting the lyric. "I don't think Ella Fitzgerald was always a deep interpreter of lyrics," wrote Michael Feinstein. "She was often inside the song, but not lyrically....Her voice was a marvelous instrument, but when it comes to certain emotional places that naturally come out of the lyric, to me she's just sometimes not there."[7] Feinstein made no mention of "I Can't Get Started," but his comments are applicable to Fitzgerald's 1956 version. He did note that Fitzgerald's earlier recordings with pianist Ellis Larkins were of high quality. A case in point is her rendition of Duke and E. Y. Harburg's "What is There to Say."

That year Bing Crosby recorded "I Can't Get Started," A superb trumpet introduction salutes Bunny Berigan and the player's fill-ins are heard throughout the song. Enter Bing whose primary goal late in his career was being Bing. By mentioning actresses Grace Kelly and Gina Lollobrigida, he seeks to be "up to date," but those references somehow date the song more than the allusions of the 1930s. Moreover, he repeatedly interjects comments between verses. After singing "Metro-Goldwyn asked me to star" he mumbles "we have to talk pay." On one occasion he actually speaks the lyric. A far cry from "Brother Can you Spare a Dime," it is all too clever, contrived, and commercial.

In 1958 Crosby recorded a duet version with Rosemary Clooney. Sammy Cahn wrote the new lyric and included a copy of it in a letter to Ira: "If there is anything at all that you object to or can improve, I would certainly be most appreciative. It is now in the hands of Sy Raidy, RCA Victor." Ira was to call him if changes were needed.[8] Crosby begins the verse, followed by Clooney. A Berigan-like trumpet introduces the chorus, and throughout it Crosby and Clooney exchange phrases that are sung with feeling. Some references are new such as "The Fourth Dimension" and "Elvis Presley" and the final stanza includes "You sum up what a gent is/ But I'm non compos mentis with you." Unfortunately, the ending is turned into a blues that is belted out by the singers. What started out as a ballad ends with a bang. What a shame. A better rendition was offered that year by pop singer Keely Smith, in large part because of Billy May's fine arrangement.

While preparing an album with Frank Sinatra, Alec Wilder asked Ira Gershwin to write a new lyric for "I Can't Get Started." What happened between the time Ira sent off the new lyric and Sinatra recorded the song is not known. But what Ira wrote did not always correspond with what Sinatra recorded. For example Ira wrote "I've flown through outer space in a plane/I've made the moon my secret domain/The Russians I've outsmarted/But can't get started with you." But Sinatra sings "Ive been around the

146

world in a plane/Designed the latest IBM brain/But lately I'm so downhearted/'Cause I can't get started with you." Ira wrote "In Cincinnati or in Rangoon I smile and gals go into a swoon/But you've got me downhearted/'Cause I can't get started with you." But Sinatra sings "In Cincinnati or in Ragoon/I simply smile and all the gals swoon/Their whims I've more than just charted/But I can't get started with you."[9] This is a clever phrase, but given Sinatra's reputation as a womanizer, it is a bit difficult to link the man with the song, to believe he could not get started with a woman. Michael Feinstein recalled that Ira found Sinatra's rendition of "I Can't Get Started" "dirgelike and lacking in the ego-deflating humor of the original."[10] But at least Sinatra included the verse and sang it as a ballad.

Feinstein has acknowledged that Sinatra was "one of the "greatest singers of the twentieth century" and noted that he had recorded two albums of songs Sinatra made famous. But he was not pleased with what Sinatra did with some lyrics: "Sinatra always said the lyric was the most important thing to him, but then he would sometimes make gratuitous changes to the words, changes that seem non-sensical."[11] For example, "Designed the latest IBM Brain" rhymes with "been around the world in a plane," but flying around the world was passé when the IBM computer was created. Although the original lyric is hardly realistic—the narrator did not settle revolutions in Spain—at least the revolution and early flight are contemporary events. Jazz trumpeter Doc Cheatham's replacement of "Greta Garbo's asked me to tea" with "Ma Rainey had me to tea," however, makes much more sense and may have actually happened. To many, Rainey may be as obscure as Garbo, but Cheatham made his first recording with the blues singer in 1926.[12] Moreover, Rainey's life was contemporaneous with the other people and events mentioned in the song.

Whether Bob Hope changed the lyric to "I Can't Get Started" on his radio and television shows as he did with his signature song, "Thanks for the Memory," is not known. But on Dean Martin's final television show of 1959, Hope joined Martin in a series of songs that Hope claimed became hits because of him, including "I Can't Get

Started." Bill Buchanan, who reviewed the show in the *Boston Daily Record*, took exception to the claim: "I balked because I remembered that Berigan recorded the song on August 7, 1937—and this was and always will be Bunny's song."[13] Late in his life, Hope acknowledged that the song may have saved his movie career. In 1930, he had an unsuccessful audition at Metro-Goldwyn-Mayer, but was called back "when they came to see me in the 'Ziegfeld Follies' singing 'I Can't Get Started With You' to this beautiful redheaded gal named Eve Arden."[14]

Whatever one thinks of these vocalizations, they contributed to making "I Can't Get Started" a standard, as did the numerous jazz players who also recorded the song during the 1950s. Pianist Paul Bley introduces the song with dissonant chords that have nothing to do with the verse. In the first chorus the melody, although modified, is recognized but during the second chorus, he slowly, with space between his phrasing, takes the song to another realm. The melody disappears, but the feeling remains that it is somewhere there. Although associated with the free jazz movement, Bley's version of "I Can't Get Started," like Lennie Tristano's, is hard to categorize. Supported by Charlie Mingus on bass and Art Blakey on drums, his interpretation seems as fresh today as when it was first released in 1952.

The same year Bley released his rendition, baritone saxophonist Gerry Mulligan and trumpeter Chet Baker launched a series of recordings that greatly impressed the jazz world. The piano-less quartet consisted of the two horns, drums and bass. Although Mulligan was from New York, to where he soon returned, and Baker was from Oklahoma, the quartet is associated with "West Coast Jazz" that emerged in California shortly after World War II and that included individuals such as Shorty Rogers, Jimmy Guiffre, Bob Cooper, Bud Shank, Shelly Manne, and others. In opposition to East Coast Jazz that emphasized long solos common of the bebop period, West Coast Jazz was highly arranged, formalized and stylized as demonstrated in octets, nonets, and tentets.

Ironically, the music offered by the Mulligan/Baker quartet harkens back, even offers a tribute, to how jazz was first played.

As Ted Gioia put it: "Not since the days of New Orleans ensemble playing had the individual members of a small combo been so willing to merge their personal sounds into a cohesive whole."[15] Schuller noted that "Gerry brought back the contrapuntal way of playing jazz into naked clarity." And he did not fall "into the obvious snare of writing classic fugues—of using the classical forms of counterpoint as a basis for his originals and arrangements. His is simply clear linear writing in jazz terms; he has shown that contrapuntal designs can swing."[16]

West Coast Jazz in general and the Mulligan/Baker quartet in particular spearheaded a chamber music approach that took jazz in a new direction, away from the big band era of mass appeal to a more intimate idiom that appealed to fewer but more serious listeners. Many of those who heard the group live appreciated the music in ways similar to those who attended classical concerts. Of all the songs the quartet recorded in 1952 and 1953, "I Can't Get Started" does not necessarily stand out from the others, but it clearly demonstrates the group's "chamber," contrapuntal style, and the mood created suggests that the musicians knew exactly what the song was all about.

Lester Young revisited the song in 1952, this time backed up by Oscar Peterson on piano, Ray Brown on base, J.C. Heard on drums, and Barney Kessel on guitar. Fortunately, Peterson, whose comping I often find intrusive, lets Kessel support Young with subtle, fluid chords. Two years later Teddy Wilson again recorded "I Can't Get Started." *Down Beat* noted that his interpretations of four standards were some of his best on record: "Its all there—the unhurried ease, the taste, the beat."[17] The following year, John Lewis, leader and pianist of the Modern Jazz Quartet, recorded the song with Percy Heath on base. In a relatively uncomplicated rendition, he solos through out the entire recording, something he never did with the MJQ. That tenor saxophonist Zoot Sims may have known the lyric in his 1956 recording is implied in the emotion of longing he expresses throughout the song. His inclusion of the verse, often ignored by instrumentalists, adds much to this fine rendition.

Jazz musicians also found Duke's other songs to their liking. Those who recorded "Autumn in New York" include Bud Powell with Charlie Mingus (1953), the Modern Jazz Quartet (1953), Shelly Manne, Jimmy Giuffre and Shorty Rogers, (1954) and Dexter Gordon (1955). "April in Paris" was recorded by Thelonious Monk (1947), Bud Powell (1950), Sauter-Finegan Orchestra (1952) and Count Basie (1955) which became a hit. With apologies to the many jazz artists who cut disks of "Taking a Chance on Love," I will mention only one—Lester Young's 1956 rendition, with Teddy Wilson, Gene Ramey on bass and Jo Jones on drums.

The songs by Ira and George were revived in *An American in Paris*. Directed by Vincente Minnelli in 1951, it included "By Strauss," written in 1936 for *The Show is On*, and "I Got Rhythm," "'S Wonderful," and "Embraceable You." But "Love Is Here to Stay," sung by Gene Kelly to Leslie Caron, is the most memorable of the film. As usual, Oscar Levant provided cynical comic relief, and in a dream sequence he plays the third movement of Gershwin's "Concerto in F." Perhaps a bit too clever with camera tricks, Minnelli has him soloing at the piano, conducting, and playing every instrument in the orchestra, and at the end shaking hands with himself, as conductor and soloist. But the stunning ending of the film, an eleven minute ballet, based on Gershwin's tone poem "An American in Paris, makes up for the short comings of this segment. " This film holds up very well.

In 1954 Ira and Harold Arlen wrote "The Search is Through" for Bing Crosby in *The Country Girl*, also starring Grace Kelly. The song went nowhere, but that year, Ira produced his last hit. "The Man that Got Away" was performed by Judy Garland in *A Star is Born*. Obviously, it was written for a female singer, but when Frank Sinatra decided to record it he suggested to Ira that it be called "The Gal That Got Away." Ira agreed and other than the title he had only the ending to change: from "A one man woman looking for/The man that got away" to "A lost, lost loser looking for/The gal that got away." Ira was very pleased with the recording.[18] But again, Frank can't seem to get started.

In *Lyrics on Several Occasions*, published in 1959, Ira compiled one hundred of his songs. He acknowledged that the prose of his book was "just as difficult, bemusing, and time-consuming as, originally, its lyrics." And the way he categorized his songs, he admitted, was arbitrary. For example, he put "Words Without Music" in the same section with "The Man that Got Away" and "I Can't Get Started" was placed with "Oh, Lady, Be Good." Whether this was the best way to organize his materials may be debated but not his commentary on many of the songs. It adds up to a brief overview of his life as a lyricist for the theater and pictures. The following year, he wrote the introduction and the marginalia for *The Ira and George Gershwin Song Book,* which contains forty songs by George, with lyrics by Ira and others. His comments in the marginalia complement those made in *Lyrics*.

In both his wit is always on display, as demonstrated in his account of having three songs nominated for academy awards. "They Can't Take That Away from Me," "Long Ago and Far Away," and "The Man That Got Away" had two things in common: they all lost and each had "away" in the title. "So— away with 'away,'" he exclaimed.[19] Oscar Levant was so angry when "They Can't Take That Away from Me" lost to "Sweet Leilani," written by "Harry Owens," that he sniffed: "His music is dead, but he lives on forever."[20]

Regarding "I Can't Get Started," Ira noted in *Lyrics* that sales of the sheet music had never amounted to much, less than forty-thousand copies sold during a twenty year period. But "an early recording by Bunny Berigan—considered by jazz devotees a sort of classic in its field—may have been a challenge (or incentive) for the great number of recordings that have followed. Not a year has gone by, in the past fifteen or so, that up to a dozen or more recordings haven't been issued."[21] That Ira was not exactly a jazz buff is hinted at in his phrase "a sort of classic in its field." In fact, his "acceptance of jazz was limited," noted Michael Feinstein. Ira was not pleased with the recording by Ray Charles and Cleo Laine of *Porgy and Bess* and even less so of the jazz version by Mel Tormé and Frances Faye. "Frances should have sung Porgy and Mel should have sung Bess," he quipped.[22] Considering jazz too egotistical, he gave Feinstein all of his Art Tatum records because Tatum was a showoff who played too many notes. Regarding another pianist who played Gershwin songs at a rapid pace, Ira told Feinstein that he should receive "a ticket for speeding."[23] But after listening three times to Lee Wiley's version of "I've Got a Crush on You" in the all Gershwin album she recorded, he admitted that slower was better than faster, that the song worked better as a ballad than as an uptempo dance number as performed in *Treasure Girl*.[24]

It is not known what Ira thought of jazz singer Carmen McRae's 1955 version of "I Can't Get Started." And why in June 1966 she asked him for a female version of the song is also not understood. He sent her the lyric he had written for Nancy Walker. Only a few changes were necessary: "I'm written up in Fortune and Time" became "Each week I'm on the cover of Time." And "From Mr. Dewey—you know the Gov." became "From Rockefeller, you know the Gov." In his accompanying letter, Ira noted that upon "rereading the lyric I believe that. . . it needs the verse."[25] Why she failed to record the song remains a mystery.

Had he heard her 1955 recording, Vernon Duke probably would have approved. He would also have approved of Alex Wilder's *American Popular Song*. In 1968 he agreed to review the book in manuscript form, and in his acknowledgements, Wilder noted that Duke "loved American music deeply and his affection was reflected in the astonishing scope and depth of his knowledge. Only weeks before his death he took the time to write a careful commentary on the concept and general scheme, of the present project, suggesting certain correctives in early theater music. Then quite suddenly, this book lost an expert and sympathetic guide."[26] Duke had died on January 16, 1969. A few days later, Ira and Lee Gershwin telegraphed his wife: "We too are heart broken and send you our deepest sympathy."[27]

Although well known and respected by his contemporaries, at the time of his death, Duke's fame, like his health, had been in decline. Nevertheless, the *New York Times* noted the event with an extensive biography of his life.[28] A Boston paper pointed out that he had composed dozens of classical works but was better known for such popular songs as "April in Paris" and "Autumn in New York." Those who appreciate classical music "knew him as Vladimir Dukelsky, the Russian-born composer of symphonies, concertos and the Diaghilev-produced ballet 'Zepher and Flora'…. He used the name Duke for his popular songs, musical shows and movie scores. 'Taking a Chance on Love' and 'I Can't Get Started With You' were among his longest-lasting songs."[29]

A year and a half after his death, Ben Bagley released *Vernon Duke Revisited.* Since 1960, the promoter had attempted to put together a tribute to Duke, but record companies thought Duke's name not well enough known to sell. Baglely, who considered Duke the greatest composer of theater music, persisted and got several stage and screen personalities to participate in the project. The result is an album that includes many of Duke's lesser known songs, such as "Round About," "Just Like a Man," "Low and Lazy," "If You Can't Get the Love You Want," and "Water Under the Bridge." Movie actress/singer Gloria DeHaven sings "Words without Music," and stage actors Tammy Grimes and Anthony Perkins perform "Now" with the feeling the song deserves. Because each song is performed by a different person, the album lacks continuity, but at least it gives the public a glimpse of Duke's genius.

Why so few of Duke's songs became standards is a question yet to be fully answered. That he spent too much of his time composing both popular and serious music was part of it, but so was bad luck and poor decision-making. During the mid-1940s, he wrote the scores for three musicals with incomprehensible librettos that closed out of town, and even those that made it to Broadway soon shut down. Because some of the songs from these shows were published and thus available to the public, however, the closings fail to answer the question. A more logical and simpler explanation is that their melodies and harmonies, products of a classically-trained composer, were too odd for the general public that after World War II became increasingly contented with the trite and trivial. And because of their complexity, most singers, pop and jazz, shied away from them.

In *American Popular Song*, Wilder acknowledged Duke's musical contributions: "For although he was born in another culture, his absorption of American popular music writing was phenomenal. One never was aware in his songs of his not being rooted in this culture, as I was, for example, when I listened to the theatre songs of Kurt Weill."[30] Nevertheless, Wilder is critical of Duke for not breaking "out of the framework of popular music forms. . . .He has kept to the conventional forms and thirty-two measure lengths, and even when he does write a complex melody, such as *Born too Late*, he doesn't move out of the framework more than melodically." Wilder was puzzled "that a schooled composer who has written a body of complex concert music should have been the man least inclined to experiment in popular forms."[31] But as explained by Arron Ziegel, "given how Duke stretches the boundaries of popular songwriting with a classically hued harmonic and melodic style, the standard formal structure needed to remain intact in order to help preserve a popular song's generic identity."[32] To be added is that Duke, like all composers for musicals, did not have the freedom to experiment radically with structure but had to write songs for particular persons in distinct situations. He had to work within the thirty-two bar framework.

That he created such innovative melodies within that framework is further testimony to his genius. As explained by Barry Singer:

> THERE is something so improbably consoling about the sadness at the heart of the best Vernon Duke melodies. This redemptive afterglow could be a consequence of sheer melodic sophistication. Duke knew how to construct a song, elegantly, with surpassing craft and harmonic flair. Yet the earned wisdom behind the sadness in his music transcends flair and craft and goes beyond sophistication.
>
> It's not that the songs are even inherently unhappy. 'Autumn in New York,' 'April in Paris,' and 'I Can't Get Started'—to name Duke's most identifiable trio—inhabit an emotional realm uncommon in the

American popular song canon, that of dry-eyed ballads of unusual poignancy. The melancholy induced by these songs, while hauntingly seductive, is never glum. . . .

Ultimately, though, Vernon Duke wrote music for grownups. His songs sang most majestically about ambivalence, not the uplift that Tin Pan Alley consumers overwhelmingly preferred. His probing melodies brought out wonderfully melancholic resonances in lyricists who were by nature, if only on the page, rather jolly—Ira Gershwin, Ogden Nash and even Yip Harburg.[33]

By this time, with film musicals in decline, there was not much work for Hollywood songwriters. With the help of Lawrence D. Stewart, Ira directed most of his attention to collecting and organizing all the materials of George's life to be deposited in the Gershwin Archives at the Library of Congress. In 1958, Stewart and Edward Jablonski published *The Gershwin Years*, a massive undertaking that includes a comprehensive biography, and numerous photographs, drawings, and documents scanning the lives of the brothers.

In their preface to the 1973 second edition, the authors acknowledge the importance of Ira's career after the death of George. For example, they went into considerable detail in describing Ira's contribution to the 1964 Billy Wilder film, *Kiss Me, Stupid*, to which he provided three revised satirical songs George had written years before. Also acknowledged were the lyrics Ira wrote for composers Harold Arlen, Aaron Copland, Jerome Kern, Burton Lane, Arthur Schwartz, Harry Warren and Kurt Weill, lyrics that "incited a redefinition of the genius of Ira Gershwin (who maintains the word is applicable only to his brother). That he is one of the great lyricists of American song is obvious—it was evident early in the joint career of the Gershwins and before. That it went generally unheralded for so long is one of the curiosities of our musical history."[34]

Composer, conductor, arranger and jazz pianist André Previn noted that Ira was "responsible for the most erudite, most romantic, and wittiest lyrics ever written" but he like most lyricists wanted them sung as written. Previn recalled an occasion when he and Ira were listening to "'S Wonderful" on an album by Frankie Laine. Once the band finished a short introduction, Laine began with "It's wonderful, it's marvelous." But "that's not right," exclaimed Ira. "If I had wanted to say 'It's wonderful,' I would have written 'It's wonderful.' I know the word 'it's.'" At the coda, when Laine repeated "it's wonderful, it's marvelous," Ira turned to Previn, looking sad and perplexed, and said: "He's done it again."[35] He was less bothered, however, when "I Got Rhythm" was changed to "I've Got Rhythm." In *Lyrics on Several Occasions*, he explained in some detail why he used "got," but concluded that "I've got nothing against 'I've got' since the verse end with 'Look at what I've got.'"[36]

He was pleased in August 1972 when he tuned on The Mike Douglas Show, to watch Benny Goodman playing "Oh, Lady, Be Good," amazed that a song written in 1924 was still being performed. And perhaps he was cheered up if and when he learned that two movies staring two "Jacks" featured "I Can't Get Started." The song was included in the score of the 1973 film *Save The Tiger*, starring Jack Lemon, and is heard in one scene in 1974's *Chinatown*, with Jack Nicholson. Ira's response might have been something about hitting the jackpot.

But he would not have been pleased with Maynard Ferguson's big band recording of the song that year. After he screeches an introduction, Ferguson, a trumpet virtuoso, sings in a casual way that clashes with the band's modern chords. A reviewer considered him a fine jazzman but was disenchanted with his singing: "Most any old misty-eyed jazz fan will tell you that the Ira Gershwin-Vernon Duke ballad was the trademark and almost personal property of the late Bunny Berigan, if not completely for horn, certainly for vocalizing."[37]

To Rosemary Clooney's credit, in 1977 she issued another recording of the song in the album *Everything's Coming up Rosie*, this time with five jazz musicians, including Nat Pierce on piano, Scott Hamilton on tenor sax, and Bill Berry on trumpet. She offers a sensitive rendition of the male version and is supported with nice fill-ins and a solo by Berry, until the blues ending robs the song of its poignancy, as it did with the duet version. Two years later she again teamed up with Hamilton and with Warren Vaché on coronet and other jazz musicians to record *Rosemary Sings the Lyrics of Ira Gershwin*, a fine album. When Michael Feinstein played Ira a demo of the album, he expected a quip but got instead "I loved every word." That line was put on the dust jacket.[38]

In 1977, Ira had hired Feinstein to first organize his record collection and later to sort out a host of materials. His closet was full of 78rpm records, test pressings production discs, aluminum air checks from radio shows in the early thirties, sixteen-inch transcription discs, and reel-to-reel tapes. Feinstein worked with Ira until he died peaceably on August 17, 1983, at eighty-six years of age. Those years are recounted in detail in Feinstein's *Nice Work If You Can Get It* and *The Gershwins and Me*.

Ira's obituaries were more like tributes. Jerry Cohen took three columns to praise the man and his music. Surviving his brother's death by forty-six years, Ira's lyrics "enhanced the enchantments of such melodists as Harold Arlen, Vernon Duke, Jerome Kern, Harry Warren, Vincent Youmans, Sigmund Romberg and Kert Weill." He wrote "more than 700 songs to tunes used in more that 30 memorable stage shows and 20 enduring films." And decades later "most are as fresh as the day they emerged from the fertile minds of Ira Gershwin and his musical partners." Cohen quoted what composer Johnny Green said about Ira: "He was very soft-spoken. But one of the great wits. He just said things that were hysterically funny. He was a master of the light touch. Even in his sentimental songs, he never dissembled sentimentality. . . .He and George in their musicals were the first explosive step—they went right smack dab into the sound of America in the American musical theater. He's been here and he's left a living legacy. He'll often be imitated. He's irreplaceable you know."[39]

Many years after Ira's death, historian of the musicals Ethan Mordden noted that wit had become a lost art: "Modern musicals that create humor within their vocal portion tend to be either generic throwbacks... or shows set in the past. . . .It's all but admitting that the present is witless, that only old forms or old times require (or deserve) the application of intelligent wordplay and ironic imagery. But the Golden Age was also clever in ballad, when Ira could somersault around Vernon Duke's rich harmonic idiom and rhythmic élan."[40]

Whether the songs by George and Ira and the other great composers and lyricists of the past had a future was discussed in 1988 at a conference at the University of Colorado, Boulder. Ben Sidran noted "We don't have dinosaurs anymore. Why? Because the climate changed. . . .Years ago, a song went out on a sort of a grapevine and it really determined how a lot of people felt or thought. The cultural climate is no longer conducive to the survival of songs as we knew them." Leonard Feather pointed out that during the past twenty years fewer and fewer quality songs had been written: "People don't think in terms of standards." But all was not lost. He cited "I Can't Get Started" as a song that had survived. After mentioning that it was introduced by Bob Hope in a Broadway show, he emphasized that it was "immortalized on a record by Bunny Berigan, and today, 53 years later, is being played and sung more often than ever."[41] The song can be heard in a scene in the 1989 movie *Blaze*, about Louisiana Governor Earl Long's affair with a stripper, staring Paul Newman and Lolita Davidovich. The song is especially relevant because the recording is by the great New Orleans soprano saxophonist Sidney Bechet, with Teddy Buckner on trumpet.

As the song continued to be recorded it also received the attention of musical scholars. In 1972, Alec Wilder analyzed its structure in *American Popular Song*. And in 1993, Robert Kimball edited *The Complete Lyrics of Ira Gershwin* containing over seven hundred songs, including published, unpublished, and revised versions of "I Can't Get Started." Apparently unaware of its evolution, Kimball considered it one "of the wittiest of all comic love songs."[42] Philip Furia seriously probed the song in *The Poets of Tin Pan Alley,* (1990) and in *Ira Gershwin: The Art of the Lyricist* (1996).

In 1997, PBS broadcast "Ira Gershwin at 100: A Celebration at Carnegie Hall." Clips from home movies and feature films complemented the live performances of a host of guests. Historian and biographer Garry Giddins, considered Rosemary Clooney's rendition of "A Foggy Day," the highlight of the evening: "For the first time all night, one found oneself thinking about the song and remembering the tribute was to Ira, not George. Backed by a big band, she was the only performer who injected the serene lilt of jazz, substituting the spaciousness of swing and her particular veracity for the rampant narcissism that preceded her. The audience roared."[43] If Ira's reputation had slipped a bit over the years, it certainly had been restored by the end of the 1990s.

In 1998 the legacy of Vernon Duke's got a boost of its own. Opera diva Dawn Upshaw recorded an album of Duke's familiar and obscure songs. On most of them she is supported by a symphony orchestra, but on the rhythm song "I Like the Likes of You" she is joined by jazz singer/guitarist John Pizzarelli. Backed up with piano, bass and drums, they swing. Of special interest is "Water Under the Bridge," with a piano and clarinet arrangement adapted from Duke's recording of 1934. She ends the album with "Ages Ago."

In January 1999 Stephen Holden of the *New York Times* heard Upshaw sing many of the songs from the album at Joe's Pub. He noted that Duke had introduced a "refined impressionism" into the popular song "that was as adventurous as anything composed by his renowned song writing peers" and that "Upshaw was an ideal interpreter of his work, since her careful balance of precisions and breeziness matches the composer's in so many ways." Holden considered "Water Under the Bridge," a high point.[44]

According to Barry Singer, also of the *Times*, Upshaw was the "only opera diva on the scene today with a classic pop singer's gift for phrasing and a torch singer's emotional fearlessness. . .to take on the full range of Duke's songwriting talent. His bittersweet chromaticism, unexpected key modulations and dense harmonies are all sung with a crystalline simplicity that eloquently illuminated Duke's darker side."[45] Upshaw received a MacArthur Foundation ("Genius Award"), in part for her recording of Duke's songs. The Foundation noted that Upshaw "is breaking down stylistic barriers and forging a new model of a performer who is directly involved in the creation of contemporary music."[46] Duke would have been pleased, because in his "dual" musical life he too broke down "stylistic barriers."

In 1999, Encores' musicals-in-concert series presented the *Ziegfeld Follies of 1936* without props and costumes. The production came about after an exhaustive search that had begun a decade earlier to locate the music, lyric sheets, and sketches, but only one full score was located—the orchestration of "I Can't Get Started." Thus, of all the songs performed on the cast recording, this one presents the best example of what the original sounded like. Peter Scolari took the role of Bob Hope, Christine Ebersole that of Eve Arden.

Peter Marks reviewed the revue, noting "Ira Gershwin's sharp lyric aptly gives a kind of shape to this effervescent, attenuated mishmash of a revue. . . . A list of what this period showcase is not could, in fact, fill pages. It is not, for instance, uproariously funny, gloriously tuneful or drenched in glamour. . . . Yet it was a swell idea of Encores to bring back the Ziegfeld Follies. Despite a dearth of the intoxicating highs one has come to expect from this exquisitely produced concert series of old musicals, Mark Waldrop's production of the songs by Vernon Duke and Gershwin and the sketches by Gershwin and David Freedman represents a fascinating evening of time travel. Thanks to newsreels, movies and musicals like "Funny Girl". . . theatergoers have an inkling of what the Follies were like. But to appreciate the impact of the Ziegfeld style more fully—its influence can be sensed today in everything from television sketch comedy to music videos—there is no substitute for the kind of warts-and-all immersion that Encores provides."[47]

Of all the songs written for the *Ziegfeld Follies of 1936*, only "I Can't Get Started" became a "standard," a term first introduced in

1937 in an article called "The Slang of Jazz" in the journal *American Speech*. As then defined, a standard was simply a song that has stood the test of time. Regardless of its musical merits, however, a song from Broadway, Hollywood, or Tin Pan Alley could become well known only through the efforts of promoters, publishers and performers. But most songs, even those that became hits, never became standards. Asking why some songs became standards while others did not is, therefore, perhaps asking the unanswerable, but opinions have been ventured.

Writing partners Young and Young have distinguished the difference between a hit which tends to be short-lived and is usually associated with a particular performer and a standard which is often performed by various musicians while still maintaining its popularity and longevity. Standards "insinuated themselves into the nation's consciousness by virtue of lyrics, melody, and the overall quality of composition." And even though "A fickle public often does not recognize greatness at the moment, but usually redeems itself by virtue of continuing sheet music and record sales."[48] The "fickle public," however, may tire of a standard. Hoagy Carmichael's "Star Dust" is not nearly as popular today as it was during the 1930s, '40s, and '50s.

According to William G. Hyland, once a "Darwinian process" had winnowed out the best of the song writers, standards could be written, "but achieving popularity was still a leisurely process. Until the rise of movie musicals, a song seeped into the public conscious; it might be heard sporadically and then more often, but eventually its durability could be measured in years, indeed, over an entire generation. The better songs became enshrined as 'standards.' They could be played and sung any time, anywhere."[49] If, however, only the "fittest" composers survived the process of "natural selection" then no second-rate or unknown tunesmith ever got lucky and wrote a standard. But this often happened. Ben Bernie, certainly not a member of the pantheon of great song writers, wrote "Sweet Georgia Brown." And not all songs took years or a generation to become a standard. "Thanks for the Memories," was written and introduced in 1937, won the academy award in 1938 and was quickly recorded by numerous artists.

In trying to understand why a song became a standard, Max Wilk became a bit unnerving: "The best approximation I've been able to unearth is that something indefinable in the music or the lyric manages to pluck at a nerve inside the listener. Somehow, it induces a response. When enough of those nerves respond, people remember the song, and the chances are good that they'll make it into a success."[50] The survival of "I Can't Get Started," however, may have resulted more from serendipity than the plucking of nerves. Without Duke casually mentioning to Ira that he had a song he might like to dabble with, the song probably would have disappeared for ever. Without it being part of a charming sketch, it could easily have been dropped from the revue. And without its publication, it may never have reached the musicians playing at the Famous Door. Yet it became a standard.

As explained by Michael Feinstein: "A song might survive because it's interpreted by a great artist. . . .It might live on after one stunning interpretation that sets a new benchmark, or it might gain new life after being rediscovered by a contemporary artist."[51] Arguably, "I Can't Get Started" meets these requirements: Bunny Berigan's rendition set a new benchmark that in turn led numerous artists—vocalists and instrumentalists—to rediscover and reinterpret the song.

In conclusion, it should be pointed out that because this process continues to the present, there is really no end to the ending of this book. Come to think of it, "No End to the Ending" could well be a melancholy song by Vernon Duke with, of course, a poignant lyric by Ira Gershwin.

Endnotes

Chapter I

1. Kenrick, *Musical Theater*, 52-56.

2. Ibid., 98-99.

3. Knapp, *The American Musical*, 29-30.

4. Jablonski, *Gershwin*, 15-16.

5. Kenrick, *Musical Theater*, 108-110.

6. Hamm, *Irving Berlin Songs from the Melting Pot*, 175.

7. Ibid., 180-81.

8. Bergreen, *As Thousands Cheer*, 59.

9. Rosenberg, *Fascinating Rhythm*, 19.

10. Furia, *Irving Berlin: A Life in Song*, 41.

11. Bergreen, *As Thousands Cheer*, 39-40.

12. Rosenberg, *Fascinating Rhythm*, 38-39.

13. Green, *Encyclopedia of the Musical Theater*, 463-64.

14. Dinerstein, *Swinging the Machine*, 198.

15. Ibid., 189, 194.

16. Green, *Encyclopedia of the Musical Theater*, 465.

17. Dinerstein, *Swinging the Machine*, 186.

18. Quoted in ibid., 184.

19. Green, *Encyclopedia of the Musical Theater*, 463.

20. DeLong, *Pops: Paul Whiteman, King of Jazz*, 59.

21. Chilton, *Who's Who in Jazz*, 351-52.

22. Quoted in Goldberg, *George Gerwhwin*, 130.

23. Quoted in ibid., 150, 151.

24. Schuller, *Early Jazz*, 63.

25. Gioia, *The History of Jazz*, 33.

26. Latrobe, *The Journals of Benjamin Henry Latrobe*, 204.

27. Schuller, *Early Jazz*, 25.

28. Gioia, *The History of Jazz*, 137-38.

29. Schuller, *Early Jazz*, 63-64.

30. Sargeant, *Jazz, Hot and Hybrid*, 137-38.

31. Riis, *Just Before Jazz*, xxi.

32. Quoted in Sullivan, "Shuffle Along," 41.

33. Schuller, *Early Jazz*, 86.

34. Vagoda, *The B. Side*, 39.

35. Young and Young, *Music of the Great Depressions*, 17-21.

36. Douglas, *Listening In*, 83-87.

37. Ibid., 86-93

38. Ibid., 97.

39. Shaw, *The Trouble with Cinderella*, 200.

40. Gioia, *The History of Jazz*, 51.

41. Ibid., 59-66.

42. Schuller, *Early Jazz*, 149-50.

43. Schuller, *The Swing Era*, 167.

44. Gioia, *The History of Jazz*, 66.

45. Ibid., 161-62.

46. Schuller, *Early Jazz*, 316.

47. Schuller, *The Swing Era*, 3-6.

48. Gioia, *The History of Jazz*, 136.

49. Friedwald, *Stardust Memories*, xiii-xiv.

50. Schuller, *The Swing Era*, 5, n3.

51. Young and Young, *Music of the Great Depression*, 40, 229.

52. Schuller, *The Swing Era*, 6-9.

53. Ibid., 5. n3.

54. Shaw, *The Trouble With Cinderella*, 334.

55. Furia, *The Poets of Tin Pan Alley*, 183.

56. Wilder, *American Popular Song*, 56-57.

57. Vagoda, *The B Side*, 48-49.

58. Duke, *Listen Here*, 268.

59. Maher, "Introduction," in Alec Wilder, *American Popular Song*, xxxi.

60. Thomas, *Harry Warren and the Hollywood Musical*, 7

Chapter 2

1. Duke, *Passport to Paris*, 7-8.

2. Ibid., 8.

3. Ibid, 37-38, 45.

4. Ibid., 48.

5. Ibid., 53, 57

6. Ibid., 61-62.

7. Ibid., 64-65.

8. Ibid., 66.

9. Ibid., 77-78.

10. Ibid., 84.

11. Ibid., 87.

12. Ibid., 88-94.

13. Ibid., 102.

14. Ibid., 103-104.

15. Vernon Duke to George Gershwin, n.p. May 25, 1924. Vernon Duke Collection, Music Division, Library of Congress.

16. Duke, *Passport to Paris*, 104.

17. Quoted in Ibid., 123-24.

18. Vernon Duke to George Gershwin, Monte Carlo, August 4, 1924, Vernon Duke Collection, Music Division, Library of Congress.

19. Quoted in Duke, *Passport to Paris*, 152-53.

20. Ibid., 217-18.

21. Ibid., 159-60.

22. Ibid., 177.

23. Ibid., 182.

24. Vernon Duke to George Gershwin, London, May 24, 1927, Vernon Duke Collection, Music Division, Library of Congress.

25. Duke, *Passport to Paris*, 206

26. Gershwin, *Lyrics on Several Occasions*, 246-47.

27. Duke, *Passport to Paris*, 218.

28. Vernon Duke to George Gershwin, n.p., n.d., (late 1929), Vernon Duke Collection, Music Division, Library of Congress.

29. Vernon Duke to George Gershwin. n.p., n.d. (different letter, late 1929) ibid.

30. Vernon Duke to George Gershwin, Boston, January 1, 1930. ibid.

31. Vernon Duke to George Gershwin, New York, n.d. (c1930), ibid.

32. Vernon Duke to George Gershwin, Philadelphia, n.d. (c1930), ibid.

33. Duke, *Passport to Paris*, 234.

34. Vernon Duke to George Gershwin, April 23, 1930, Vernon Duke Collection, Music Division, Library of Congress.

35. Duke, *Passport to Paris*, 237.

36. Ibid., 238-41.

37. Ibid., 242-45.

38. Ibid., 265.

39. Ibid., 267-68.

40. Quoted in Wilk, *They're Playing Our Song*, 233.

41. W.E.G., "Walk a Little Faster," *Boston Herald*, November 19, 1942.

42. Ibid, 277.

43. *Dallas Morning News*, February 3, 1935.

44. Quoted in Duke, *Passport to Paris*, 277.

45. Ibid., 278.

46. Ibid., 285.

47. Kenrick, *Musical Theater*, 210.

48. Wilder, *American Popular Song*, 358-60.

49. Duke, *Passport to Paris*, 292.

50. Ibid, 302.

51. Wilder, *American Popular Song*, 361.

52. Furia, *Poets of Tin Pan Alley*, 207.

53. *Boston Herald*, April 22, 1934.

54. *Greensboro Daily News*, September 27. 1935.

Chapter 3

1. Schwartz, *Gershwin: His Life & Music*, 3-7.

2. Ibid., 4-5.

3 Ira Gershwin, "My Brother," in Armitage, ed, *George Gershwin*, 16-17.

4. Furia, *Ira Geshwin: The Art of the Lyricist*, 1-4.

5. Quoted in ibid., 4.

6. Ibid., 7.

7. Ibid., 10, 23-25.

8. Quoted in Rosenberg, *Fascinating Rhythm*, 31.

9. Ibid.,19.

10. Furia, *Ira Gershwin*, 28-29.

11. Ibid., 30-38.

12. Gershwin, *Lyrics on Several Occasions*, 4.

13. Ibid., 173.

14. Feinstein, *The Gershwins and Me*, 58.

15. Gershwin, *Lyrics on Several Occasions*, 111.

16. Ibid., 252-53.

17. Parker, *Dorothy Parker Stories*, 76-77.

18. Gershwin, *Lyrics on Several Occasions*, 342.

19. Rosenberg, *Fascinating Rhythm,* 190.

20. Ibid.

21. Crawford, "George Gershwin's 'I Got Rhythm' (1930)," 58-60.

22. Gershwin, *Lyrics on Several Occasions,* 31

23. Ibid., 271.

24. Ibid., 234.

25. *New York Times,* October 15, 1930.

26. Ibid., November 9, 1930.

27. Ibid.

28. Furia, *The Poets of Tin Pan Alley,* 3.

29. Tormé, *My Singing Teachers,* 112-13.

30. Feinstein, *The Gershwins and Me,* 179-81.

31. Sondheim, *Finishing the Hat,* xxvii.

32. Gershwin, *Lyrics on Several Occasions,* 323.

33. Goldberg, *George Gershwin,* 198-99.

34. Gershwin, "Words and Music," *New York Times,* November 9, 1930.

35. Rosenberg, *Fascinating Rhythm,* xix.

36. *New York Times,* November 9, 1930.

37. Gershwin, *Lyrics on Several Occasions,* 120.

38. Levant, *A Smattering of Ignorance,* 203-204.

39. Gershwin, *Lyrics on Several Occasions,* 41-42.

40. *New York Times,* January 19, 1930.

41. Kenrick, *Musical Theater: A History,* 222.

42. Sondheim, *Finishing the Hat,* 176.

43. Gershwin, *Lyrics on Several Occasions.,* 351-52.

44. Furia, *Ira Gershwin,* 95.

45. Bruccoli, F. Scott Fitzgerald: *A Life In Letters,* 408, n.1.

46. Quoted in Furia, *Ira Gershwin,* 118.

47. Sondheim, *Finishing the Hat,* 176.

48. Ibid.

49. Duke, *Passport to Paris,* 308.

50. Ibid.

51. *Greensboro Daily News,* October 20, 1935.

52. Duke, *Passport to Paris,* 315-16.

53. Gershwin, *Lyrics on Several Occasions,* 100.

Chapter 4

1. Gioia, *The History of Jazz*, 135.

2. Young and Young, *Music of the Great Depression*, 68.

3. Laufe, *Broadway's Greatest Musicals*, 31-36.

4. Kenrick, *Musical Theatre*: 209; Jones, *Our Music, Ourselves*, 83.

5. Jones, *Our Music, Ourselves*, 84.

6. *New Yorker Volkszeitung*, October 28, 1930.

7. *Plain Dealer* March 7, 1932.

8. *San Diego Union*, May 25, 1939.

9. Furia, *Irving Berlin: A Life in Song*, 131.

10. *Times-Picayune*, July 14, 1933.

11. Young and Young, *Music of the Great Depression*, 47-48.

12. Quoted in Gorney, *Brother Can You Spare a Dime?* 12.

13. Quote in Wilk, *They're Playing Out Song*, 230-31

14. Harburg, "From the Lower East Side to 'Over the Rainbow,'" 145.

15. Young and Young, *Music of the Great Depression*, 49.

16. Furia, *The Poets of Tin Pan Alley*, 204-205.

17. Giddins, *Bing Crosby: A Pocketful of Dreams*, 305.

18. Davis, *The Craft of Lyric Writing*, 61.

19. Young and Young, *Music of the Great Depression*, 34.

20. Tormé, *My Singing Teachers*, 48-49.

21. Duke, Liner Notes, *Andre Previn Plays Songs by Vernon Duke*, 3.

22. Wilder, *American Popular Song*, 361.

23. Furia, *The Poets of Tin Pan Alley*, 14-15.

24. *Boston Herald*, November 26, 1939.

25. Wilder, *American Popular Song*, 363.

26. Mantooth, *The Best Chord Changes*, 64-65.

27. Kimball, ed., *The Complete Lyrics of Ira Gershwin*, 254-255.

28. Feinstein, *The Gershwins and Me*, 160-61.

29. Gioia, *The Jazz Standard*, 156.

30. *Plain Dealer*, August 19. 1988.

31. Furia, *The Poets of Tin Pan Alley*, 144.

32. Ibid., 165-66.

33. Feinstein, *Nice Work If You Can Get It*, 218.

Chapter 5

1. Green, *Encyclopedia of the Musical Theatre*, 8, 21, 179.
2. *New York Times*, May 10, 1936.
3. Green, *Encyclopedia of the Musical Theatre*, 15.
4. Duke, *Passport to Paris*, 311-12.
5. *Boston Herald*, December 25, 1935.
6. Duke *Passport to Paris*, 310-311.
7. *Boston Herald*, January 5, 1936.
8. Kimball, ed., *The Complete Lyrics of Ira Gershwin*, 243.
9. Ibid., 259.
10. Duke, *Passport to Paris*, 316.
11. Gershwin, *Lyrics on Several Occasions*, 194-95.
12. *Boston Herald*, December 31, 1935.
13. Duke, *Passport to Paris*, 316.
14. Kimball, ed., *The Complete Lyrics of Ira Gershwin*, 244-45.
15. Gershwin, *Lyrics on Several Occasions*, 53.
16. *Greensboro Daily News*, February 1, 1936.
17. *New York Times*, January 31, 1936.
18. Duke, *Passport to Paris*, 315-16.
19. Ibid., 311.
20. Kimball, ed., *The Complete Lyrics of Ira Gershwin*, 254.
21. Stewart, "Constructing the Follies," 12.
22. Ibid.
23. Furia, *Ira Gershwin*, 130.
24. Kimball, ed., *The Complete Lyrics of Ira Gershwin*, 246.
25. Furia, *Ira Gershwin*, 130-31.
26. Gershwin, *Lyrics on Several Occasions*, 246.
27. Goldberg, *George Gershwin*, 189-90.
28. Kimball, ed., *The Complete Lyrics of Ira Gershwin*, 254-55.
29. Mordden, *Sing For Your Supper*, 139.
30. Duke, *Passport to Paris*, 317.
31. *Time*, February 10, 1936.
32. Modden, *Sing For Your Supper*, 139.
33. *New York Times*, February 10, 1936.
34. Ibid., January 31, 1936.
35. Baker, *Josephine*, 101-102.

36. Rose, *Jazz Cleopatra*, 166.

37. *San Francisco Chronicle*, April 4, 1936.

38. Vernon Duke to Ira Gershwin, n.p., October 21, 1936, Vernon Duke Collection, Music Division, Library of Congress.

39. *New York Times*, September 15, 1936.

40. Ira Gershwin to Vernon Duke, Beverly Hills, October 6, 1936, Ira Gershwin Collection, Music Division, Library of Congress.

41. Vernon Duke to Ira Gershwin, New York, October 21, 1836, Vernon Duke Collection,

42. ibid.

43. *Evening Star*, May 11, 1937.

44. *Evansville Courier and Press*, October 31, 1937.

45. Ibid., November 13, 1937.

46. *Greensboro Record*, November 3, 1937.

47. Hamm, *Irving Berlin Songs from the Melting Pot*, 17.

48. Sudhalter, *Lost Chords*, 501-502.

Chapter 6

1. Quoted in Dupuis, *Bunny Berigan*, 120.

2. Condon, *We Called It Music*, 240-41.

3. Kay Halle in Jablonski, ed., *Gershwin Remembered*, 88.

4. Quoted in Dupuis, *Bunny Berigan*, 124.

5. Dupuis, *Bunny Berigan*, 120-121.

6. Chilton, "Bunny Berigan," 5-9.

7. Ibid., 9-18.

8. *Boston Herald*, June 26, 1942.

9. Sudhalter, *Lost Chords*, 502.

10. Schuller, *The Swing Era*, 471-73.

11. *Metronome*, January 1937, 21.

12. Schuller, *The Swing Era*, 473, 474.

13. Dupuis, *Bunny Berigan*, 291.

14. Sudhalter, *Lost Chords*, 509.

15. Gioia, *The Jazz Standard*, 157.

16. Dupuis, *Bunny Berigan*, 290.

17. Schuller, *The Swing Era*, 471.

18. Vernon Duke to Ira Gershwin, Boston, October 5, 1937, Vernon Duke Collection, Music Division, Library of Congress.

19. Quoted in *Down Beat*, September 1, 1941.

20. Chilton, "Bunny Berigan," 3, 26.

21. Maddocks, "Billy Holiday," 6-7.

22. Ibid., 10-22.

23. Giddins, *Visions of Jazz*, 371-72.

24. Maddocks, "Billy Holiday," 44.

25. Schuller, *The Swing Era,* 539.

26. Ibid., 542.

27. *Life*, April 17, 1939, 11, 72.

28. Hildegarde, *Over 50—So What!* 1-33, 161-172

29. Duke, *Passport to Paris*, 349-50.

30. Quoted in Wilk, *They're Playing Our Song,* 198.

31. Schinnerling, Liner Notes, *Ginny Simms: One More Dream.*

32. Torme, *My Singing Teachers*, 86.

33. Spellman, "Art Tatum," 10-11.

34. Ibid., 15-16.

35. Levant, *A Smattering Of Ignorance*, 195-96.

36. Spellman, "Art Tatum," 16-17.

37. Levant, *A Smattering Of Ignorance*, 196.

38. Spellman, "Art Tatum," 17.

39. Gelles, "Teddy Wilson," 9.

40. Ibid., 9-11.

41. Ibid., 13-19.

42. Ibid., 19-22

43. Schuller, *The Swing Era,* 502.

44. Ibid., 503.

45. McDonough, "Lester Young," 6-20.

46. Schuller, *The Swing Era*, 554-55.

47. Maggin, *Dizzy*, 93.

48. Gioia, *The History of Jazz*, 155-56.

49. Edward A. Wolpin to Ira Gershwin, New York, March 12, 1943, Ira Gershwin Collection, box 47, folder 21, Music Division, Library of Congress.

50. No author, Liner Notes, *V-Disk: A Musical Contribution by America's Best for Our Armed Forces Overseas.*

51. Friedwald, *Jazz Singing*, 211-12.

52. Ibid., 209.

53. Clark, *Wishing on the Moon*, 429.

54. Matzorkis, "Ben Webster," *Giants of Jazz*, 8-20.

55. John Chilton, "Notes on the Music," in Matzorkis, "Ben Webster," *Giants of Jazz*, 49-50.

56. Friedwald, *Jazz Singing*, 85-88.

57. *New York Times*, December 12, 1975.

58. Friedwald, *Jazz Singing*, 84.

59. Tormé, *My Singing Teachers*, 49.

60. Gus Kuhlman, Liner Notes, *Lee Wiley*, "On The Air, Volume 2.

61. Schuller, *The Swing Era*, 692.

62. Sudhalter, *Lost Chords*, 571-89, 598-600.

63. Schuller, *The Swing Era*, 693.

64. Shaw, *The Trouble with Cinderella*, 331.

65. Crawford, "George Gershwin's 'I Got Rhythm' (1930)," 67-68.

66. Maggin, *Dizzy*, 93.

67. Ibid., 165.

68. Quoted in Shipton, *Groovin' High*, 162.

69. Maggin, *Dizzy*, 165.

70. Shipton, *Groovin' High*, 162.

71. Shim, *Lennie Tristano*, 1-31.

72. *Metronome*, March, 1948.

73. Ibid., August 1949.

74. *Down Beat*, March 12, 1947.

75. *Metronome*, April 1947.

76. Shim, *Lennie Tristano*, 36.

77. Schuller, *The Swing Era*, 840.

78. Ibid., 841.

79. Gioia, *The History of Jazz*, 250.

Chapter 7

1. Quoted in Rosenberg, *Fascinating Rhythm*, 323.

2. Gershwin, *Lyrics on Several Occasions*, 248.

3. *Boston Herald*, November 12, 1936.

4. Gershwin, *Lyrics on Several Occasions*, 65-66.

5. Gioia, *The Jazz Standards*, 117.

6. Duke, *Listen Here*, 260-61.

7. Ira Gershwin to Vernon Duke, Beverly Hills, October 6, 1936. Ira Gershwin Collection, Music Division. Library of Congress.

8. Vernon Duke to Ira Gershwin, New York, October 21, 1936, Vernon Duke Collection, ibid.

9. Ira Gershwin to Vernon Duke, Beverly Hills, May 5, 1937, Ira Gershwin Collection Ibid.

10. Merle Armitage, "Preface," in Armitage, ed., *George Gershwin*, n.p.

11. Duke, *Passport to Paris*, 352.

12. Ira Gershwin to Vernon Duke, Beverly Hills, December 8, 1938, Ira Gershwin Collection, Music Division, Library of Congress

13. Ferde Grofe, in Armitage, ed., *George Gershwin*, 29.

14. George Antheil, in ibid., 119.

15. Erma Taylor, in ibid., 179.

16. David Ewen, in ibid, 207.

17. Feinstein, *Nice Work If You Can Get It*, 79.

18. Friedwald, *Stardust Memories*, 189.

19. *New York Times,* November 14, 1937.

20. Gershwin, "Marginalia on Most of the Songs," in Gershwin, Glaser, and Sirmay, *The George George and Ira Gershwin Song Book*, xiv.

21. Vernon Duke to Ira Gershwin, New York, December 3, 1938, Vernon Duke Collection, Music Division, Library of Congress.

22. Vernon Duke to Ira Gershwin, New York, February 16, 1940, ibid.

23. *New York Times,* December 29, 1940.

24. Mordden, *Beautiful Mornin'* 46.

25. Wilder, *American Popular Song*, 366.

26. Duke, *Passport to Paris*, 392.

27. *New York Times,* October 26, 1940.

28. Ibid., May 28, 1943.

29. Gershwin, *Lyrics On Several Occasions*, 186.

30. Ibid., 275.

31. Ira Gershwin to Vernon Duke, Beverly Hills, October 6, 1947. Ira Gershwin Collection, Music Division, Library of Congress.

32. *San Diego Union*, May 1, 1946.

33. *Boston Herald,* July 4, 1944.

34. Duke, *Passport to Paris*, 424-29.

35. *Plain Dealer,* November 19, 1944.

36. Duke, *Passport to Paris,* 478-79.

37. Ibid., 480.

38. *State Times Advocate,* January 15, 1953.

39. Mordden, *Anything Goes,* 13-14.

40. Duke, Liner Notes, *Songs by Bobby Short.*

41. Duke, *Passport to Paris,* 3.

42. Ibid, 3-4.

43. Duke, *Passport to Paris,* 484.

44. *New York Times,* March 27, 1955.

45. Ira Gershwin to Vernon Duke, n.p., March 29, 1955. Ira Gershwin Collection, Music Division, Library of Congress.

46. Quoted in *Richmond Times Dispatch,* May 16, 1955.

47. Scott Dunn, ed., *The Vernon Duke Songbook,* 1-3.

48. Duke, Liner Notes, *André Previn Plays Songs by Vernon Duke.*

49. Vernon Duke to Ira Gershwin, n. p. October 2, 1959, Vernon Duke Collection, Music Division, Library of Congress.

50. Gershwin, *Lyrics on Several Occasions,* 246-47.

51. Duke, Liner Notes, March 24, 1959, *Barney Kessel Modern Jazz Performance from Bizet's Carmen.*

52. Quoted in Holden, "The "Adventures and Battles" of Vladimir Dukelsky," 317, 318.

53. Mordden, *Open a New Window,* 85.

54. Duke, *Listen Here,* 246-50.

55. Ibid., 272.

56. Ibid., 28-29.

57. Duke, Liner Notes, *Andre Previn Plays Songs by Vernon Duke,*

58. *Down Beat,* February 10, 1966, 34-35.

59. *Richmond Times Dispatch,* September 1, 1963.

60. *Down Beat,* February 10, 1966, 34-35.

Chapter 8

1. Ira Gershwin to Vernon Duke, October 6, 1947, Ira Gershwin Collection, Music Division, Library of Congress.

2. *Metronome,* September 1948, 22-23.

3. Schuller, *Musings,* 107-108.

4. Tormé, *My Singing Teachers,* 197.

5. Feinstein, *Nice Work If You Can Get It.* 98.

6. Ibid., 287.

7. Feinstein, *The Gershwins and Me*, 205.

8. Sammy Cahn to Ira Gershwin, n.p. August 5, 1958, The Ira Gershwin Collection, box 47, folder 21, Music Division, Library of Congress.

9. Ira Gershwin Lyric of "I Can't Get Started" for Frank Sinatra, ibid.

10. Feinstein, *The Geshwins and Me*, 237.

11. Ibid, 207.

12 . *New York Times*, June 3, 1997.

13. *Boston Daily Record*, May 4, 1959.

14. *Los Angeles Times*, February 1, 1987.

15. Gioa, *West Coast Jazz*, 174.

16. Quoted in Hentoff, *Jazz Is*, 121.

17. *Down Beat*, June 16, 1954, 12.

18. Gershwin, *Lyrics On Several Occasions*, 243.

19. Ibid., 48.

20. Quoted in Feinstein, *Nice Work If You Can Get It,* 39.

21. Gershwin, *Lyrics On Several Occasions,* 100.

22. Feinstein, The Gershwins and Me, 216.

23. Feinstein, *Nice Work if You Can Get It*, 122.

24. Gershwin, *Lyrics on Several Occasions,* 94-95.

25. Ira Gershwin to Carmen McRae, n.p., June 21, 1966, Ira Gershwin Collection, box 47, folder 21, Music Division, Library of Congress.

26. Wilder, "Acknowledgements," *American Popular Song,* xvi.

27. Ira and Lee Gershwin to Mrs Vernon Duke, Western Union Telegram, January 20, 1969. Box 41, folder 21,Ira Gershwin Collection, Music Division, Library of Congress.

28. *New York Times*, January 18, 1969.

29. *Boston Record American,* January 19, 1969.

30. Wilder, *American Popular Song,* 357.

31. Ibid., 368.

32. Ziegel "One Person, One Music," 332.

33. *New York Times*, January 24, 1999.

34. Jablonski and Stewart, *The Gershwin Years,* 18.

35. Quoted in Previn, *No Minor Chords,* 104.

36. Gershwin, *Lyrics on Several Occasions,* 343.

37. *Richmond Times Dispatch*, October 27, 1974.

38. Feinstein, *Nice Work If You Can Get It,* 99-100.

39. *Oregonian,* August 18, 1983.

40. Mordden, *Sing For Your Supper,* 139.

41. *Plain Dealer,* August 19, 1988.

42. Kimbell, *The Complete Lyrics of Ira Gershwin,* xvii.

43. Gary Giddins, *Visions of Jazz,* 600.

44. *New York Times,* January 25, 1999.

45. Ibid., January 24, 1999.

46. Ibid., September 25, 2007.

47. Ibid., March 27,1999.

48. Young and Young, *Music of the Great Depression,* 40-42, 45.

49. Hyland, *The Song Is Ended,* 292.

50. Wilk, *They're Playing Our Song,* 28.

51. Feinstein, *The Gershwins and Me,* 254.

Bibliography

Documentary Sources

Ira Gershwin and Vernon Duke Collections, Music Division, Library of Congress.

Newspapers and Periodicals

Boston Daily Record, 1959.

Boston Herald, 1932, 1934, 1935, 1936, 1944.

Cleveland Plain Dealer, 1932.

Dallas Morning News, 1931, 1935.

Down Beat, 1937, 1941, 1954, 1966.

Evansville Courier and Press, 1937.

Greensboro Daily News, 1935.

Greensboro Record, 1937.

Life, 1940.

Los Angeles Times, 2014.

Metronome, 1941.

New York Times, 1930-1999.

New York Times Magazine, 2016.

Richmond Times Dispatch, 1955, 1963.

San Diego Union, 1946.

San Francisco Chronicle, 1941.

Springfield Union. 1955, 1959, 1963, 1965.

State Times Advocate, 1933.

Time, 1936.

Times-Picayune, 1933.

Published Sources

Armitage, Merle, Editor and Designer. *George Gershwin*. New Introduction
      by Edward Jablonski. First Published in 1938 by Merle Armitage and
      Walter Burroughs. New York: Da Cap Press, Inc., 1995.

Baker Josephine and Jo Bouillon. *Josephine*. Translated from the French by
      Mariana Fitzpatrick. New York, Hagerstown, San Francisco,
      London: Harper & Row, Publishers, 1977.

Bergreen, Laurence. *As Thousands Cheer: The Life of Irving Berlin*. New York:
      Penguin Books, 1990.

Bruccoli, Mathew, ed. *F. Scott Fitzgerald: A Life in Letters*. London and New York:
      Simon & Schuster Inc., 1994.

Chilton, John. "Bunny Berigan." *Giants of Jazz*. Alexandria, Virginia: Time Life
      Records, 3-26.

_____. *Who's Who in Jazz: Storyville to Swing Street*. Philadelphia: The Chilton
      Book Company, 1972

Clarke, Donald. *Wishing on the Moon: The Life and Times of Billie Holiday*. New
      York: Penguin Books, 1994.

Collier, James Lincoln. *Louis Armstrong: An American Genius*. New York: Oxford
      University Press, 1983.

_____. *The Making of Jazz: A Comprehensive History*. New York: Dell Publishing
      Company, 1978.

Condon, Eddie. Narration by Thomas Sugrue. *We Called It Music: A Generation of
      Jazz*. New York: Henry Holt and Company, 1947.

Crawford, Richard, "George Gershwin's 'I Got Rhythm' (1930)." In Robert Wyatt
      and John Andrew Johnson, editors, *The Gershwin Reader*. Oxford and
      New York: Oxford University Press, 2004, 156-172.

Davis, Sheila. *The Craft of Lyric Writing*. Cincinnati, Ohio: Writer's Digest Books,
      1985.

DeLong, Thomas A. *Pops: Paul Whiteman, King of Jazz*. New Jersey: New Century
      Publishers, 1983.

Dinerstein, Joel. *Swinging the Machine: Modernity, Technology, and African-
      American Culture Between the World Wars*. Amherst & Boston: University
      of Massachusetts Press, 2003.

Douglas, Susan. *Listening in: Radio and the American Imagination*. Minneapolis and
      London: University of Minnesota Press, 2004.

Duke, Vernon. Liner Notes, September, 10, 1958. *Andre Previn Plays Songs by Vernon Duke.* Ocean New   Jersey: Musical Heritage Society, Inc. 1992.

———. Liner Notes, March 24, 1959. B*arney Kessel: Modern Jazz Performances from Bizet's Carmen.* Contemporary Records, 1986.

———. Liner Notes, *Songs By Bobby Short*, n.d. Atlantic Recording Corporation, 2004

———. *Listen Here! A Critical Essay on Music Depreciation.* New York: Ivan Obolensky, Inc., 1963.

———. *Passport to Paris.* Boston and Toronto: Little, Brown and Company, 1955.

Dunn Scott, ed. *The Vernon Duke Songbook.* Milwaukee: Boosey & Hawkes, 2012.

Dupuis, Robert. *Bunny Berigan: Elusive Legend of Jazz.* Baton Rouge and London: Louisiana State University Press, 1993.

Ewen, David. *American Songwriters: An H. W. Wilson Biographical Dictionary.* New York: The H. W. Wilson Company, 1987.

Feinstein, Michael. *Nice Work If You Can Get It: My Life in Rhythm and Rhyme.* New York: Hyperion, 1995.

———, with Jan Jackman. *The Gershwins and Me: A Personal History in Twelve Songs.* New York: Simon & Schuster, 2012.

Freedland, Michael. I*rving Berlin.* New York: Stein and Day, 1974.

Friedwald, Will. *Jazz Singing: America's Great Voices From Bessie Smith to Bebop and Beyond.* New York: Macmillan Publishing Company, 1990.

———. *Stardust Melodies: The Biography of Twelve of America's Most Popular Songs.* New York: Pantheon Books, 2002.

Furia, Philip. *Ira Gershwin: The Art of the Lyricist.* New York and Oxford: Oxford University press, 1996.

———. Irving Berlin: *A Life in Song.* New York: Schirmer Books, 1998.

———. *The Poets of Tin Pan Alley: A history of America's Great Lyricists.* Second Edition. New York and Oxford: Oxford University Press, 1991.

Gelles, George. "Teddy Wilson." *Giants of Jazz.* Alexandria, Virginia: Time-Life Records, 3-26.

Gershwin, Ira. *Lyrics on Several Occasions.* First published in 1959. London: Elm Tree Books/Hamish Hamilton, 1977.

_____, "Marginalia on Most of the Songs," in Ira Gershwin, Milton Glaser and Dr. Albert Sirmay. *The George and Ira Gershwin Song Book.* New York: Simon and Schuster, Inc., 1960.

_____. "Words and Music." *New York Times,* November 9, 1930.

Giddins, Gary. *Bing Crosby: A Pocketful of Dreams, The Early Years, 1903-1904.* Boston, New York, London: Little, Brown and Company, 2001.

_____. *Visions of Jazz: The First Century.* Oxford University Press, 1998.

Gillespie, Dizzy and Al Fraser. *To be, or Not. . .to Bop.* First Published in 1979. Minnesota: University of Minnesota Press, 2009.

Gioia, Ted. *The History of Jazz.* New York and Oxford. Oxford University Press, 1997.

_____. *The Jazz Standards: A Guide to the Repertoire.* Oxford and New York: Oxford University Press, 2012.

_____. *West Coast Jazz: Modern Jazz in California, 1845-1960.* New York and Oxford: Oxford University Press, 1992.

Goldberg, Isaac. Supplement by Edith Carson. *George Gershwin: A Study in American Music.* New York: Frederick Ungar Publishing Company, 1958.

Goldberg, Mark Trent. "Deconstructing the Follies." In *Ziegfeld Follies of 1936,* A Decca Broadway Cast Album. City Center Encores, 14-18.

Gorney, Sondra K. *Brother Can You Spare A Dime? The Life of Composer Jay Gorney.* London, Maryland, Toronto, Oxford: The Scarecrow Press, Inc., 2005.

Green, Stanley. *Encyclopedia of the Musical Theatre.* New York: Dodd, Mead & Company, 1976.

_____. *Broadway Musicals: Show by Show.* Milwaukee: Hall Leonard Books, 1985.

Griffin, Mark. *A Hundred or More Hidden Things: The Life and Films of Vincente Minnelli.* Philadelphia: Da Capo Press, 2010.

Grossman, Barbara W. *Funny Woman: The Life and Times of Fanny Brice.* Bloomington and Indianapolis: Indiana University Press, 1991.

Hamm, Charles. *Irving Berlin Songs from the Melting Pot: The Formative Years, 1907-1914.* New York: Oxford University Press, 1977.

Haney, Lynn. *Naked at the Feast: A Biography of Josephine Baker.* New York: Dodd, Mead & Company, 1981.

Harburg, E. Y. "From the Lower East Side to 'Over the Rainbow.'" *In Creators and Disturbers: Reminiscences of Jewish Intellectuals of New York Drawn from Conversations with Bernard Rosenberg and Ernest Goldstein.* New York: Columbia University Press.

Hentoff, Nat. *Jazz Is.* New York: Limelight Editions, 1984.

Hildegarde. With Adele Whitely Fletcher. *Over 50—So What!* Garden City New York: Doubleday & Company, 1963.

Holden, Scott. "The "Adventures and Battles" of Vladimir Dukelsky (a.k.a. Vernon Duke." *American Music,* Vol. 28, No. 3 (Fall: 2010): 297-319.

Hyland. William G. *The Song Is Ended: Songwriting and American Music, 1900-1950.* Oxford, New York, Toronto: Oxford University Press, 1995.

Ind, Peter. *Jazz Visions: Reflections on Lennie Tristano and His Legacy.* London: London, Equinox Publishing Ltd., 2005.

Jablonski, Edward. *Gershwin.* New York" Doubleday, 1987.

_____, ed. *Gershwin Remembered.* Portland, Oregon: Amadeus Press, 1992.

_____, and Lawrence D. Stewart. *The Gershwin Years.* New York: Doubleday & Company, 1973.

Jones, John Bush, *Our Musicals, Ourselves: A Social History of the Musical Theatre.* Hanover and London: Brandeis University Press. Published by the University Press of New England, 2003.

Jones, Max. *Jazz Talking: Profiles, Interviews, and Other Riffs on Jazz Musicians.* First Published in 1987. New York: Da Capo Press, 2000.

Kenrick, John. *Musical Theatre: A History.* New York: The Continuum International Publishing Group, Inc., 2008.

Kimball, Robert, ed. *The Complete Lyrics of Ira Gershwin.* New York: Alfred A. Knopf, 1993.

Knapp, Raymond. *The American Musical and The Formation of National Identify.* Princeton and Oxford. Princeton University Press, 2005.

Kuhlman, Gus. Liner Notes. *Lee Wiley, On the Air.* Vol. 2. Redmond, Washington: Totem Records, 1979.

Latrobe, Benjamin. *The Journals of Benjamin Henry Latrobe, 1799-1820: From Philadelphia to New Orleans,* Vol. 3. Edited by Edward C. Carter II, John C. Van Horne and Lee W. Formwalt. New Haven: Yale University Press, 1980.

Laufe, Abe. *Broadway's Greatest Musicals*. Revised Edition. New York: Funk & Wagnalis, 1977.

Levant, Oscar. *A Smattering of Ignorance*. New York: Garden City publishing Co. Inc., 1942.

Maddocks, Melvin. "Billy Holiday." *Giants of Jazz*. Alexandria, Virginia: Time-Life Records, 3-30.

Maggin, Donald L. *Dizzy: The Life and Time of John Birks Gillespie*. New York: Harper Collins, 2005.

Maher, James T. "Introduction," in *Alec Wilder, American Popular Song: The Great Innovators, 1900-1950*. New York: Oxford University press, 1972, xxiii-xxxix.

Maltin, Leonard. *The Great American Broadcast: A Celebration of Radio's Golden Age*. New York; Dutton, 1907.

Mantooth, Frank. *The Best Chord Changes for the Most Requested Standards*. Milwaukee: Hal Leonard Corporation, 1990.

Matzorkis, Gus. "Ben Webster." *Giants of Jazz*. Alexandria, Virginia: Time-Life Records, 3-30.

McDonough, John. "Lester Young." *Giants of Jazz*. Alexandria, Virginia: Time-Life Records, 3-28.

Metlzer, Milton. *Brother, Can you Spare a Dime? The Great Depression, 1929-1933*. New York: Knopf, 1969.

Miller, Scott. *Rebels with Applause: Broadway's Groundbreaking Musicals*. Portsmouth, N.H.: Heinemann, 2001.

Mongan, Norman. *The History of the Guitar in Jazz*. New York: Oak Publications, 1983.

Mordden, Ethan. *Anything Goes: A History of American Musical Theatre*. Oxford and New York. Oxford University Press, 2013.

_____. *Beautiful Mornin': The Broadway Musicals in the 1940s*. New York and Oxford: Oxford University Press, 1999.

_____. *Open a New Window: The Broadway Musicals of the 1960s*. New York: Palgrave for St Martin's Press, 2001.

_____. *Sing for Your Supper: The Broadway Musicals of the 1930s*. New York: Palgrave McMillan, 2005.

Morella, Joseph, and George Mazzei. *Genius and Lust: The Creative and Sexual Lives of Cole Porter and Noel Coward*. New York: Carroll & Graf Publishers, Inc., 1995.

O'Meally, Robert G. "An Appreciation of Armstrong's Hot Five and Seven Recordings." *Louis Armstrong: The complete Hot Five and Hot Seven Recordings*. New York: Sony Music Entertainment Inc., 2000.

Panassé, Hugues. *The Real Jazz*. Translated by Anne Sorelle Williams. New York: Smith & Durell Inc., 1942.

Parker, Dorothy. *Dorothy Parker Stories*. New York, Avenel, New Jersey. Wings Books, 1992.

Paul, Elliot, *That Crazy American Music*. Indianapolis and New York: The Bobs-Merrrill Company, Inc., 1957.

Previn, André. *No Minor Chords: My Days in Hollywood*. New York and London: Doubleday, 1991.

Riis, Thomas L. *Just Before Jazz: Black Musical Theater in New York, 1890-1915*. Washington and London: Smithsonian Institution Press, 1989

Rose, Phyllis. *Jazz Cleopatra: Josephine Baker in her Time*. New York, London, Toronto, Sydney, Auckland, Doubleday, 1989.

Rosenberg, Deena. *Fascinating Rhythm: The Collaboration of George and ira Gershwin*. New York: Dutton, 1991.

Schinnerling, Lares. Liner Notes, *Ginny Simms: One More Dream*. Flare Records, 2006.

Schuller, Gunther. *Early Jazz: Its Roots and Musical Development*. New York: Oxford University Press, 1968.

_____. *Musings: The Musical Worlds of Gunther Schuller*. New York and Oxford: Oxford University Press, 1986.

_____. *The Swing Era: The Development of Jazz, 1930-1945*, New York and Oxford: Oxford University press, 1989.

Schwartz, Charles. *Gershwin: His Life & Music*. New York and Indianapolis: Bobbs-Merrill Company, 1973.

Shaw, Artie. *The Trouble With Cinderella: An Outline of Identity*. First Published in 1952. New York: Da Capo Press, 1979.

Shim, Eunmi. *Lennie Tristano: His Life In Music*. Ann Arbor: The University of Michigan Press, 2007.

Shipton, Alyn. *Groovin' High: The Life of Dizzy Gillespie.* New York and Oxford: Oxford University Press, 1999.

Sobchack, Thomas and Vivian C. Sobchack, *An Introduction to Film.* Boston and Toronto: Little, Brown and Company, 1980.

Sondheim, Stephen. *Finishing the Hat.* New York: Alfred A. Knopf, 2010.

Spellman, A. G. "Art Tatum." *Giants of Jazz.* Alexandria, Virginia: Time-Life Records, 3-14.

Stewart, Lawrence D. "Constructing the Follies," In *Ziegfeld Follies of 1936, A Decca Broadway Cast Album.* City Center Encores, 9-13.

Sudhalter, Richard M. *Lost Chords: White Musicans and Their Contribution to Jazz, 1915-1945.* New York and Oxford: Oxford University Press, 1999.

Sulllivan, John Jeremiah. "American Shuffle." *New York Times Magazine,* March 27, 2016, 32-41, 53-55.

Thomas, Tony. *Harry Warren and the Hollywood Musical.* Secaucus, New Jersey: Citadel Press, 1975.

Tormé, Mel. *My Singing Teachers: Reflections on Singing Popular Music.* New York and Oxford: Oxford University Press, 1994.

Vagoda, Ben. *The B Side: The Death of Tin Pan Alley and the Rebirth of the Great American Song.* New York: Riverhead Books, 2015.

Whitcomb, Ian. *Irving Berlin and Ragtime America.* London: Century Hutchee, 1987.

Winthrop, Sergeant. *Jazz, Hot and Hybrid.* Third Edition. New York: Da Capo Press, 1976.

Wilder, Alec. *American Popular Song: The Great Innovators, 1900-1950.* Edited and Introduced by James T. Maher. New York: Oxford University Press, 1972.

Wilk, Max. *They're Playing Our Song: The Truth Behind the Words and Music of Three Generations.* Mount Kisco, New York and London: Moyer Bell Limited, 1991.

Wilson, John S. *The Collector's Jazz: Traditional and Swing.* Philadelphia and New York: J. B. Lippincott Company, 1955.

Young, William H., and Nancy K. Young. *Music of the Great Depression.* Westport, Connecticut and London: Greenwood Press, 2005.

Ziegel, Aaron. "One Person, One Music: Reconsidering the Duke-Dukelsky Musical Style." *American Music,* Vol. 28, No. 3 (Fall: 2010): 320-345.

Index

Lang, Eddie, 6
Latouche, John, 127
Lee, Gypsy Rose, 86
Leslie, Edgar, 87
Leslie, Lew, 59
Levant, Oscar, 27, 49, 106, 133, 150, 151
Lewis, John, 149
Lillie, Beatrice, 123
Linn, Ray, 115
Lombardi, Clyde, 118, 120
Lombardo, Guy, 17
Lunceford, Jimmie, 16
Lyman, Abe, 111
Manne, Shelly, 117, 138, 148, 150
Manone, Wingy, 112
Martin, Dean, 147
Martin, Mary, 131
Matthews, Roger, 11
May, Billy, 146
McDonough, Dick, 93
McEvoy, J. P., 45
McHugh, Jimmy, 56
McKenzie, Red, 91, 92, 93, 94, 97, 99
McLane, Ralph, 38
McRae, Carmen, 152
Mercer, Johnny, 97, 126, 127
Merman, Ethel, 45, 56
Meth, Max, 128
Millinder, Lucky, 116
Miller, Glenn, 111
Miller, Marilyn, 6
Mingus, Charlie, 148, 150
Minnelli, Vincente, 72, 75, 79, 123, 129, 130, 133, 150
Monk, Thelonious, 116, 150
Morton, Jelly Roll, 11, 13, 108

Moten, Bennie, 15, 109
Moten, Benny, 112
Moten, Etta, 58
Mulligan, Gerry, 148, 149
Nash, Ogden, 132, 155
Nicholas, Fayard, 73, 86
Nicholas, Herold, 73, 86
Nichols, Red, 45, 115
Niesen, Gertrude, 73, 74, 76, 79, 86
Noone, Jimmie, 11
O'Connell, Hugh, 73, 86
O'Day, Anita, 145
Oliver, King, 11, 13, 14, 107
Original Dixieland Jazz Band, 11
Ory, Kid, 11, 14
Oumansky, Alexander, 26
Owens, Harry, 151
Page, Walter, 15, 100
Parker, Charlie, 116, 126
Parker, Dorothy, 34, 44
Perelman, S. J., 35, 132
Perkins, Anthony, 153
Peterson, Oscar, 144, 149
Pettiford, Oscar, 116, 117
Phillips, Flip, 144
Phillips, H. I., 72
Pickins, Jane, 86, 87
Pierce, Nat, 157
Pizzarelli, John, 159
Porter, Cole, 18, 56, 62, 68, 70, 80, 104, 113
Powell, Bud, 150
Powell, Eleanor, 129
Powell, Mel, 121
Preisser, Cherry, 73
Preisser, June, 73

About The Author

George Harwood Phillips began his intellectual journey with a B.A. in English in 1959 from what was then San Diego State College. After teaching one year at El Capitan High School in Lakeside, California he was accepted to the Teachers to East Africa Program and spent two years at Mpwapwa Secondary School in Tanzania. Before returning to the States, he taught for a semester at the American high school on the Torejon Airforce Base in Madrid, Spain.

He received his Ph.D. in history from the University of California, Los Angeles in 1973 and went on to teach at the University of the West Indies in Jamaica, the University of California, Los Angeles and the University of Colorado at Boulder. During his years at Colorado, he received a visiting research fellowship at Edith Cowen University in Perth, Australia and was the holder of the Rupert Costo Chair in American Indian History at the University of California, Riverside. He is the author of eight books on Native Americans in California history.

Although a jazz buff since high school and a student of the jazz guitar, only after retiring from Colorado in 1996 did he find time to write about the music he has studied and listened to in clubs, at concerts, and on records for so many years. His next project is a biography of Vernon Duke.

COYOTE HILL PRESS

www.ingramcontent.com/pod-product-compliance
Lightning Source LLC
Chambersburg PA
CBHW071958090426
42740CB00011B/1989